KV-590-858

Contents

Parents and schools

Customers, managers or partners?

Edited by
Pamela Munn

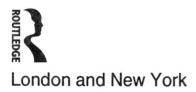

London and New York

First published 1993
by Routledge
11 New Fetter Lane, London EC4P 4EE

Simultaneously published in the USA and Canada
by Routledge
29 West 35th Street, New York, NY 10001

© 1993 Pamela Munn

Typeset in Baskerville by LaserScript, Mitcham, Surrey
Printed and bound in Great Britain by
Biddles Ltd, Guildford and King's Lynn

British Library Cataloguing-in-Publication Data
A catalogue record for this book is available from the British Library.

ISBN 0–415–07692–7
0–415–08926–3 ✓

Library of Congress Cataloging in Publication Data
Parents and schools: customers, managers or partners?/
    edited by Pamela Munn.
    p. cm. – (Educational management series)
    Includes bibliographical references and index.
    ISBN 0–415–07692–7. – ISBN 0–415–08926–3 (pbk.)
    1. Education – Great Britain – Parent participation.
    2. Home and school – Great Britain. 3. School, Choice of – Great
Britain.
I. Munn, Pamela. II. Series.
LC225.33.G7P36   1993
370.19'31'0941 – dc20   92-28832
                                                              CIP

Parents have been given new rights over their children's schooling. They now have the right to choose the school their children will attend and to be involved in school management through membership of school governing bodies in England and Wales, and school boards in Scotland. These new rights are intended to make schools more responsive to parental concerns. Operating in a climate where market forces are believed to be a powerful way of bringing about school improvements, the enhanced role for parents in school affairs has important implications for the quality of schooling. This book considers the new roles of customer and manager now being assigned to parents and asks what the consequences are for schools. Will better schools be the result? How will traditional parent–teacher relationships be affected? What role remains for local education authorities? The book brings together contributions from distinguished writers in the field of education policy and practice. Drawing on the disciplines of policy studies, educational research and philosophical enquiry, the book presents a unique opportunity to consider parental involvement in schooling from a range of perspectives. It will appeal to those interested in home–school relations, in educational governance and in comparing British policy in these areas with that in Europe.

Pamela Munn has a long-standing research interest in home–school relations. School accountability to parents and parental involvement in school management are particular interests. She is currently joint director of an ESRC-funded project on the comparative effects of devolved management of schools in England and Scotland. Depute Director of the Scottish Council for Research in Education, she has published widely on the functioning of school boards in Scotland.

Educational management series
Edited by Cyril Poster

Contributors

Michael Adler is Reader in Social Policy and a member of the Centre for Educational Sociology at the University of Edinburgh. He is author, with Alison Petch and Jack Tweedie, of *Parental Choice and Educational Policy* (Edinburgh University Press, 1989). With Pamela Munn and Charles Raab, he is currently researching the devolved management of schools in England and Scotland, a project funded by the Economic and Social Research Council.

John Bastiani is Lecturer in Education at the University of Nottingham. He has a long-standing interest in parental involvement in education and has published widely on the subject. He was a member of the team on the Home–School Contract of Partnership project 1989–92 sponsored by the Royal Society of Arts and the National Association of Head Teachers.

Michael Golby is Reader in Education at the University of Exeter. His main interests lie in school governorship and he has been responsible for a series of research projects investigating the roles of governing bodies and their impact on schools. He has recently established a network to compare and contrast the functions of governing bodies and their equivalents in Western European countries.

Seamus Hegarty is Deputy Director of the National Foundation for Educational Research. He has published widely on the education of children with special needs and has a particular interest in the problems and possibilities of the integration of children with special needs into mainstream schooling.

Ruth Jonathan is Head of the Department of Education at the University of Edinburgh. She has taught, researched and published extensively on educational philosophy and policy. Her major areas of interest are equity issues: in education and vocationalism, in differentiation and selection and in market mechanisms for educational distribution, in all of which she focuses on the conflicts between individual freedoms and social justice. She is currently Chairman of the Philosophy of Education Society of Great Britain.

Alastair Macbeth is Senior Lecturer in Education at the University of Glasgow. He has written extensively on parental involvement in schools and has undertaken major research projects on parental choice of schools and on Scottish school councils. He is currently adviser to the European Parents' Association.

Pamela Munn is Depute Director of the Scottish Council for Research in Education. School accountability to parents and parental involvement in school management are particular interests. She has published widely on the functioning of school boards in Scotland and has recently completed a small study of parents' values in education.

Charles Raab is Senior Lecturer in the Department of Politics at the University of Edinburgh. Among his publications on education policy are (with Andrew McPherson) *Governing Education: A Sociology of Policy since 1945* (Edinburgh University Press, 1988) and a number of articles and contributions to books. He is a member of the Centre for Educational Sociology and serves on the International Advisory Board of the *Journal of Education Policy*.

Sally Tomlinson is the Goldsmiths' Professor of Policy and Management in Education at Goldsmiths' College, London. Her particular interests lie in ethnic minorities and schooling. She has published widely on multicultural education as well as focusing on the particular issues of home–school relations. Recently, with S. Hutchinson, she completed a study of Bangladeshi parents and education in the London Borough of Tower Hamlets.

Foreword

'Parental voice opens up . . . greater possibilities for school improvement than parental choice.' Pamela Munn's words encapsulate much of the thinking behind this well-researched book. It is a timely challenge to the muddled thinking in government circles and elsewhere which fails to take in the fact that for many parents choice is phantasmagorical.

The Scottish Council for Research in Education (SCRE) has an outstanding record of practical involvement with educational issues that affect schools, their pupils and the parents. It is good to see the writings of those who work in or with the SCRE in this field on the role of parents in relation to the management of schools given the wide readership that books in this series are currently enjoying.

As an educationist working closely with schools and local education authorities (LEAs) on management issues, I see clearly the value of every one of these chapters for the improved relationship with parents that is not only a legal requirement but is also keenly desired by most of our schools. There are, of course, those managers in schools and LEAs who are so overburdened by the weight of imposed innovations that they feel they cannot give this additional task the time and energy it demands. If there is one overriding message from this book, it is that school–parent partnership may well not, in fact, be yet another task, but rather be the easing oil that will facilitate the effectiveness of the school's work in general. Those who see only gloom and doom in what is happening in education in the early 1990s will, I hope, be heartened by the messages of these contributions.

Cyril Poster
Series editor

Acknowledgements

This book had its origins in the Edinburgh Education Policy Group, now sadly defunct. The Group provided a forum for researchers from different institutions and academic disciplines to discuss education policy issues. It speedily became apparent that policy on parental involvement in schools was a major theme of interest to many group members. Some of these are contributors to this book, namely Michael Adler, Ruth Jonathan and Charles Raab. I am grateful, therefore, to Andrew McPherson and Lindsay Paterson, Centre for Educational Sociology, University of Edinburgh for instigating the group and for carrying out the range of administrative tasks associated with it.

Education policy stems from a UK agenda but is operationalised rather differently north and south of the border. The British Educational Research Association (BERA) has set up policy task groups on school governorship and on local management of schools which provided opportunities to compare and contrast developments in these areas in England and Scotland. The role of these groups in promoting research networks is warmly acknowledged.

The Scottish Council for Research in Education (SCRE) provided a stimulating environment in which to discuss and develop ideas about parental involvement. My colleagues Colin Holroyd and Nick Arney who were researching school boards helped enormously and Table 6.2 is the result of their empirical work. Janette Finlay typed successive drafts of the text with good humour and somehow coped with software in all shapes and sizes.

Finally, I should like to acknowledge the sustained support and encouragement of my husband, Graham Munn. Not only has he tolerated substantial disruption to family life, but has also provided a sounding board for ideas and been a real 'critical friend'.

Chapter 1

Introduction

Pamela Munn

The importance of parental involvement in schools is now generally recognised. A number of studies of school effectiveness identify parental involvement as one of the key variables associated with effectiveness in general and with pupil attainment in particular. The more involved parents are with their children's schooling, the greater it seems are the chances of their children doing well. The ways in which parental involvement help children's attainment are not well-understood but some researchers have highlighted its positive effect on pupil motivation (Ekstrom *et al.*, 1988; Jaynes and Wlodkowski, 1990). Involvement can mean many things, from attending parents' evenings and school open days to helping in the classroom. There are three aspects to traditional parental involvement which are worth drawing attention to:

- it has largely concerned the well-being of the parent's own child
- it has been to support the largely taken-for-granted value system of the school
- collective action, such as through parents' or parent–teacher associations has been largely concerned with fund-raising, or transmitting information, and has not usually challenged the school's way of doing things.

The important point is that parents are generally expected to uphold school values, whether this is in ensuring their children do homework, behave in an acceptable way or come to school dressed appropriately. Parental involvement in identifying the values which the school will embody is rare. The parent's role is to reinforce school values and to support the school if there are problems with their children.

This state of affairs is one which most teachers have found comfortable. Parents who challenge school values are, like their children, typified as 'problems'. Such parents can include 'pushy' middle-class individuals who may complain that their children are not being stretched intellectually, as well as those living in areas of multiple deprivation where problems such as non-completion of homework may not be the most urgent priority for a family beset by social and economic difficulties.

Some schools, of course, have tried to extend and develop their relations with parents through experiments in home–school partnership projects, through signed understandings between home and school about the responsibilities of each or through involving parents in the classroom. The home–school contract of partnership project set up by the Royal Society of Arts (RSA) and the National Association of Head Teachers (NAHT) is a recent example of developments in Britain, while many schemes have been developed in the USA under the auspices of the Headstart programme. All these schemes acknowledge the importance of parental involvement to help schools provide a rewarding experience for pupils. Indeed, a pamphlet describing a number of schemes for parental involvement in American schools is called *The Parent Principle: Prerequisite for Educational Success* (Educational Testing Service, 1991).

Few would deny the need to involve parents in their children's schooling, although the nature and extent of that involvement as well as the factors affecting it are a matter of some debate. However, traditional notions of parental involvement in schools have been radically shaken by the education policy of the Conservative government during the 1980s. Let us look briefly at the salient features of that policy as far as parents are concerned.

NEW ROLES FOR PARENTS

The new roles ascribed to parents in a series of Education Acts north and south of the border have been developed in a climate where market forces are believed by the Conservatives to be powerful agents in bringing about school improvement and raising standards. Hence one new role for parents is that of a customer of the education service. Parents have been granted new rights to choose the school their children will attend. Since funding for schools largely depends on the numbers of pupils they attract, parental influence on schools will be enhanced, or so the theory goes. Schools will be encouraged to provide the kind of education which parents want or they will suffer the consequences of falling rolls – namely reductions in staffing levels and ultimately closure.

This major innovation of parental choice and its consequences for schools are one theme of this book. The role of parent as customer was previously confined to those who could afford to pay directly for their children's schooling and send them to private schools. Alternatively, parents who could afford to do so bought houses in the catchment areas of desirable state schools to ensure a place for their children. In the sense of making choice available to all parents, it could be argued that the legislation is equitable and fair. Certainly, parents have not been slow to take advantage of the new rights assigned to them. However, the new role for parents as customers makes a number of assumptions about schools and about parents.

Perhaps the most obvious is that a choice of school is available to parents. For many parents living in rural or semi-rural areas there is, in reality, no practical alternative to sending their child to the local school. This is particularly the case for parents of secondary school children. To provide choice for such parents a radical change in transport policy would be needed. Secondly, for those parents who have a number of schools within easy reach, the nature of the choice being offered is quite limited. The national curriculum, attainment targets and national testing signal that most schools will operate in a market whereby they offer the same product, not different products. City Technology Colleges and the Assisted Places scheme to help children from poorer families attend independent schools are attempts to diversify provision but, so far, these are on a very limited scale. Thirdly, there is an assumption that schools will be able to respond to parental concerns and so improve. Research on the operation of parental choice in Scotland, which has had radical legislation earlier than England and Wales, showed that the main criteria on which parents chose schools were geographical location, safe access, and the kind of children who already attend (Adler *et al.*, 1989). These are not criteria to which schools can easily respond. Fourthly, it is assumed that all parents are equally well-informed about their rights, and are able to exercise them.

These assumptions are addressed in this volume from different perspectives by Jonathan, Macbeth, Adler and Tomlinson. From the perspective of a philosopher of education, Jonathan poses a number of questions about parents' rights to increased choice and control over their children's schooling. She alerts us to the function of talk about rights as a 'trumping' move overriding counter-claims and dissent and describes rights of differing orders. She also alerts us to the complexities of parents exercising proxy rights on behalf of their children. Fundamentally, however, she introduces the question, also addressed by Adler, of the proper balance between individual rights and collective welfare rights in social policy.

Macbeth examines parents' rights in schooling in other parts of Europe in a wide-ranging chapter which begins with a salutory reminder that most education goes on outside school. He uses his knowledge of policy and practice in Europe to raise awareness about the assumptions we, in Britain, make about parents and schooling and to challenge these assumptions. He predicts that the European Community will become increasingly influential in school affairs and speculates that this may encourage the changes in attitude needed to bring about real parental involvement in schools, involvement which directly influences their children's educational experiences.

Adler reviews the effects of open enrolment in Scotland, drawing on two major research studies by teams in Glasgow and Edinburgh universities, to suggest that increasing inequality of provision has been the result. However, recognising the potentially beneficial effects of parental choice, he argues for increased diversity of provision as a way of protecting children's interests while retaining parents' right to choose.

Tomlinson highlights the 'gulf of misunderstanding' between ethnic minority parents and teachers and points out that racial and cultural differences add an extra dimension to home–school relationships. She reminds us just how limited the notion of parental choice can be by revealing that ten of the fifty-three Bangladeshi families in Tower Hamlets involved in a research study have had a child 'out-of-school' at some point because of insufficient places being available. Furthermore, her research suggested that Bangladeshi parents' knowledge about education, about their children's schooling and about their rights under recent legislation was poor.

The consumer role for parents is not the only one ascribed to them through recent legislation. Their rights to an increased voice in school affairs have been strengthened firstly through their increased representation on governing bodies through the 1986 Education (No. 2) Act and secondly by the extensive powers and responsibilities of governing bodies under the 1988 Education Reform Act. In Scotland, the 1988 School Boards Act set up the broad equivalent to governing bodies, though they have fewer powers than their counterparts south of the border. The ways in which these bodies are working and their potential for involving parents actively in the life of schools are discussed by Golby (England and Wales) and Munn (Scotland).

Golby discusses the role of parents as governors and sees possibilities of parent governors providing 'new recruits to the active citizenry', thereby strengthening local democracy. Underpinning such aspirations, however, are worries about representation, in terms both of the dominance of the white, middle-class male as governor and of the absence of any statutory responsibility for parent governors to keep in touch with their electors. Representation issues are also raised by Munn in her discussion of the ways in which school boards are working in Scotland and by Tomlinson who points out how few members of ethnic minorities there are on governing bodies. Governing bodies may adopt rather different roles, reflecting interpretations of their purpose, and Golby highlights some of these. In Scotland, school boards have developed in unexpected ways, ways which suggest that schooling as a collective welfare right for society as a whole is highly valued. Indeed, one of the ironies of the Scottish situation is that having created, or at least strengthened, the legitimacy of the parental voice in school affairs, government has had to live with that voice being raised in opposition to its policy on national testing in English and mathematics for pupils in Primary 4 and Primary 7.

Parents operating through local federations of governing bodies or through other interest groups are likely to assume greater importance in policy-making in education. They will, no doubt, be assiduously courted by teachers' unions, local authorities and central government as a way of seeking to legitimise policy and perhaps even be involved in the policy making process itself. Raab explores the notion of partnership in policy making in his chapter, looking at the likely role of education authorities in the future. He sees education authorities as 'down' but not 'out' in school governance and points to the costs of central government imposing control on reluctant authorities. As Lawrence Stenhouse remarked in another context, teachers who feel unjustly called to account spend their time trying to cheat the accountants, not improve the balance sheet (Stenhouse, 1977). Raab argues that a common culture is now being sought amongst the big players in education policy making, a culture which recognises and accepts new values of educational management such as performance indicators and development plans.

The new roles of customer and manager do not exclude direct contact between parent and teachers about the education of individual children and old notions of teachers and parents as partners in their children's education. The direct involvement of parents in their children's schooling is still supremely important and is addressed in different ways by Bastiani and Hegarty. Bastiani begins by exploring the idea of partnership and he outlines the legal and contractual requirements of schools in terms of partnership with parents. He gives examples of partnership in operation and suggests ways ahead for policy and practice. While Bastiani has few doubts that the notion of partnership is a helpful one (though in need of clarifying), Hegarty eschews the idea, contending that it conceals more than it reveals. Instead he opts for a functional description of the components of good home–school relations from a special needs perspective. This approach, he argues, allows for the possibility of partnership but is not dependent upon it. The five forms of home–school contact which he discusses could well form a checklist for those wanting to analyse their policy and practice in this area.

CHOICE, VOICE AND PARTNERSHIP

How do the new roles now granted to parents sit with the traditional features of home–school relations mentioned earlier? The role of the parent as consumer is congruent with the traditional parental concern for the schooling of his or her own child. It emphasises private rights and interests, not the collective welfare of children in schools. It is worth emphasising this point, because it is a good illustration of the shift in the balance between individual rights and collective welfare rights, in favour of the former, in public services. Since 1979, users of public services have been granted rights as part of a general reaction against what the government perceived to be the failure of the providers of these services to deal effectively with social problems. The Citizen's

Charter is the most recent example of this shift. In education, schools have been perceived by both Labour and Conservative governments as failing to raise standards sufficiently and to be a part of the explanation for our relative economic decline. The Conservative answer to improve performance is through the operation of parental choice in a school market. An important point to notice is that the elevation of private interest suggests that the road to higher standards will be paved with many losers. This is so both theoretically and empirically. At a theoretical level, for markets to operate, standards have to be different or there is no point in choosing. Ball (1990: 7) points out:

> It is argued that competition will raise standards. Not that standards will become equivalent between schools, [for] that would dampen the market dynamic, [and] there must be diversity in the market place.

And empirically, the major studies of the operation of parental choice in Scotland (Adler *et al.*, 1989; Macbeth *et al.*, 1986) indicated that, in the areas where choice operated, the relative disadvantage of those remaining in unpopular schools increased. Whether increasing inequality of provision will in the long run produce higher standards for all is an empirical question which cannot yet be answered. Whether it is a price worth paying is an ideological question, depending on one's view of the proper balance between individual client orientation and collective welfare orientation in public services.

Whether parents as individual customers have been able to be more involved in determining school values is not yet clear. In very popular schools where there have been more placing requests than places, it may be that schools begin to choose parents, rather than vice versa. Furthermore, as the Scottish research cited above showed, the criteria on which parents choose schools, proximity, pupil safety and the kind of children who attend, are difficult for schools to respond to. Interestingly enough, these criteria are not confined to Scottish parents. In a recent review summarising European research and opinion surveys, Macbeath and Weir (1991) highlighted accessibility, safety, the preservation of friendship groups, and local reputation for discipline and high standards of teaching as the key criteria used by parents choosing schools. This reiterates the point that responsiveness to parental concerns is not wholly within the school's power.

Parents as members of school governing bodies or school boards challenge traditional home–school relationships in two ways. Firstly, governing bodies are explicitly about the collective well-being of the school, rather than an individual parent's private interest. Secondly, they go beyond parent or parent–teacher associations in having clearly defined statutory responsibilities, which in the case of governing bodies are extensive and substantial. Responsibilities for such areas as ensuring a broad and balanced curriculum within the framework of the national curriculum, for managing the school budget, and for the hiring and firing of school staff, all open up considerable potential for influencing the school climate. It is difficult to generalise about the effects of governing bodies on schools and about parental experience of governorship. Research suggests a diversity of experience but the dominance of the head and the chair has been noted by Deem and Brehony (1990), while, in Scotland, boards have been much readier to challenge the education authority than the school (Munn 1992; Munn and Holroyd, 1989). Whether active participation in managing the schools will evolve as governors and board members gain in experience remains to be seen. It has been interesting to see local federations of boards and governing bodies take shape and, in Scotland, the emergence of the nascent national school board federation. Governing bodies and boards have promoted the idea of a collective parental interest in schools and politicised parents in a way that challenges traditional notions of home–school relations. In the long run they may be a more important vehicle for parents to exert influence than school choice.

Challenge to traditional notions of home–school partnership is also evident in the pilot schemes and experiments in home–school projects that are taking place in various parts of Britain. The many different schemes developed under the Home–School Contract of Partnership mentioned earlier are testimony to the energy, enthusiasm and commitment of parents and teachers. Their benefits are in terms of improved communication between home and school and of better opportunities for parents and teachers to support children's learning. It is, as yet, unclear whether the schemes encourage collectivist as well as individual private interest and whether schools have substantially changed their way of doing things as a consequence of increased parental involvement.

Whatever role or roles parents adopt in their relations with schools, it is clear that parents are here to stay as a force in policy making. They now have access to more and better presented information about schools than ever before and they are being wooed assiduously by all sides. In Scotland, for example, Strathclyde Region Education Authority, one of the largest in Europe, has established a Parents' Consultative Group, which has a membership of around thirty parents. The Group will meet the Director of Education on a six-weekly basis 'to discuss matters that may interest or concern them regarding the [authority's] policies' (Strathclyde Regional Council, 1992). And Scotland's largest teaching union has recently issued A Manifesto for Partnership in which close links between parents and teachers are advocated (Educational Institute of Scotland, 1992).

Whether as customers, managers or partners, parents have an important role to play in their children's schooling. This collection of papers raises issues, questions assumptions and analyses some recent developments. It begins with general chapters on issues of rights, choice, voice and partnership before focusing on the last three in more detail. Running through the contributions are questions about collective welfare and individual welfare rights, relations between the expert, and the non-expert, and school accountability. These are considered at greater length in the concluding chapter.

POSTSCRIPT

These chapters were written long before the publication of the government's White Paper Choice and Diversity: A New Framework for Schools (Department for Education and Welsh Office, 1992). The White Paper proposes extending parental choice and thus the role of parents as customers of the education service by 'simplifying the creation of grant-maintained schools and by opening the way to greater variety in education through the formation of new schools and by encouraging specialisation' (p. iii). The encouragement of the creation of greater numbers of grant-maintained schools also clearly has implications for parents as managers of such schools through their membership of governing bodies. Perhaps the most significant of the proposals contained in the White Paper is the reduction in the role of local education authorities (LEAs). This is commented upon briefly by Raab as a postscript to his chapter on the functioning of LEAs as partners in education policy making.

The White Paper cannot be analysed here but it is clear that issues of accountability, choice and school autonomy run through it – issues which are the concern of this volume. The path from White Paper to legislation and thence to implementation is seldom smooth and the impact of reforms of school governance upon the quality of teaching and learning in British schools is yet to be researched. Whatever systems of governance finally emerge, parents will continue to play a vital role in their children's learning. The contributions raise questions about the nature of that role and hope to inform debate on the nature, shape and function of Britain's schools – a debate which the White Paper is certain to encourage.

REFERENCES

Adler, M., Petch, A. and Tweedie, J. (1989) *Parental Choice and Educational Policy*, Edinburgh: Edinburgh University Press.

Ball, S. (1990) 'Education, Inequality and School Reform: Values in Crisis!' Inaugural Lecture, Centre for Educational Studies, King's College, University of London.

Deem, R. and Brehony, K. (1990) 'The Long and the Short of It' *Times Educational Supplement*, 13 July.

Department for Education and Welsh Office (1992) *Choice and Diversity: A New Framework for Schools*, London: HMSO.

Education (No. 2) Act 1986, London: HMSO.

Education Reform Act 1988, London: HMSO.

Educational Institute of Scotland (1992) *A Manifesto for Partnership*, Edinburgh: Educational Institute of Scotland.

Educational Testing Service (1991) *The Parent Principle: Prerequisite for Success*, Princeton, NJ: Educational Testing Service.

Ekstrom, R.B., Goertz, M.E. and Rock, D.A. (1988) *Education and American Youth*, Philadelphia: Falmer.

Jaynes, J.H. and Wlodkowski, R.J. (1990) *Eager to Learn: Helping Children Become Motivated and Love Learning*, San Francisco: Jossey-Bass.

Macbeath, J. and Weir, D. (1991) *Attitudes to School*, Glasgow: Jordanhill College.

Macbeth, A., Strachan, D. and Macaulay, C. (1986) *Parental Choice of School*, Glasgow: Department of Education, University of Glasgow.

Munn, P. (1992) 'Devolved Management of Schools and FE Colleges: A Victory for the Producer over the Consumer?' in Paterson, L. and McCrone, D. (eds) *The Scottish Government Yearbook 1992*, Edinburgh: Unit for the Study of Government in Scotland.

Munn, P. and Holroyd, C. (1989) *Pilot School Boards: Experiences and Achievements*, Edinburgh: Scottish Council for Research in Education.

School Boards (Scotland) Act 1988, Edinburgh: HMSO.

Stenhouse, L. (1977) 'Accountability', *Times Educational Supplement*, 13 May.

Strathclyde Regional Council (1992) 'Education Department Forms Parental Discussion Group', News Release, 15 January.

Chapter 2

Parental rights in schooling

Ruth Jonathan

In Britain, as in many areas of the industrialised world, the past decade has seen far-reaching changes in the provision of education. In England and Wales, and in Scotland, two apparently contradictory themes have characterised these changes: increased state intervention in the content and range of provision, together with increased deregulation within that range to stimulate an internal market. The avowed rationale for deregulation is that the competitive ethos created by market conditions will shake up a service hidebound by tradition, wrest control from the vested interests of professionals and bureaucrats, and promote more rapid response to the needs of society, understood as an economic entity. On its own, this rationale would be insufficient to justify a shift away from systematic local control and provision, directed towards the general welfare of the young, which prevailed throughout the decades of post-war consensus. Apart from any issues of principle, the rationale rests upon claims about the present state of education, and predictions about the effects of proposed change, which are, to say the least, questionable. There is, however, an overriding justification for deregulation which, being ideological, rests not on empirical claims which may be disputed, but on moral claims which are presented as above dispute.

That justification reflects the individualistic ethos of the 1980s, with its emphasis on consumer power and choice, together with a libertarian ethic which claims that individuals have both rights and duties to make decisions and take responsibility in areas of personal and social life where previously the state or its professionals made decisions and assumed responsibilities in the name of the public good. Government has thus presented many redirections of social policy as a championing of the individual consumer, and this is particularly the case with changes in education policy. A whole raft of policies, most obviously early legislation to permit parents to choose a child's school and the 'opting out' sections of late 1980s legislation, but also measures to diversify provision, including the Assisted Places scheme, the introduction of the Technical and Vocational Education Initiative (TVEI) and the founding of City Technology Colleges – all of these have been presented to the public as an overdue granting of the rights of parents to have more say in the choice and control of their children's schooling. In justifying policies as merely the proper granting of individual rights and freedoms, they are taken off the agenda of mundane debate about likely effects on the education system as a whole and on the general welfare it was designed to promote. Talk of rights functions, as it frequently does in social and moral debate, as a 'trumping' move (Dworkin, 1977), decreasing the weight of any dissenting view. It is, therefore, vital to examine the status of the 'trumping' procedure itself, so that important changes in educational policy are not granted immunity from ordinary evaluation in terms of general effects.

This chapter therefore addresses those questions of the rights of parents which are of concern to both parents and teachers, and which are germane to recent educational legislation. Analysis will show these matters to be far more complex and controversial than populist rhetoric suggests. A preliminary look at the status of rights in moral and legal discussion will be followed by an examination of the nature of parents' rights in general, looking at their grounding in the parents' role as trustee of a child's welfare and agent for securing its current and future interests. With a distinction maintained between rights in law and those moral rights to which we feel entitled, whether or not they are reflected in legislation, the general consideration of the rights of parents will be applied to the schooling context. At this point, further complexities will be revealed, since the granting and exercise of individual rights in a social context where the welfare of each is inseparable from the welfare of others, but where individuals are in competition with each other, raise some of the most thorny questions of ethics and of political theory.

'RIGHTS TALK' IN MORAL AND LEGAL AFFAIRS

The concept of a right developed in seventeenth- and eighteenth-century political thought to flag those individual liberties and immunities which any just system of government should not infringe. Since particular concepts of rights are predicated on views about human nature and hence about what constitutes a worthwhile life and a good society, we would expect those concepts to be neither fixed nor uncontroversial. In the contemporary world, there is general agreement that whatever is basic to the life of rational and self-conscious social beings like us should not be interfered with. Slavery, arbitrary imprisonment, and the deliberate curtailment of thought and its expression are held up as paradigm cases of the unacceptable infringement of people's rights. Beyond a central core of protected immunities, however, controversy soon develops. As the social world becomes more complex, and possible forms of individual flourishing multiply, more and more aspects of life become open to rights claims. As these also multiply, they tend to come into conflict with each other, so that fulfilling the rights claims of one individual or group may threaten to infringe the similar claims of other individuals or groups.

It is for this reason that ethical, political and legal debate has long been characterised by controversy about the usefulness of talk of rights in arbitrating in disputes which arise in the moral and social spheres, with many maintaining that 'rights-talk' constantly throws us back onto the horns of just those moral dilemmas – between liberty and equality, between the interests of the individual and those of the group, between the similar claims of competing individuals or groups – which it was invoked to resolve in the first place. Nonetheless, the history of rights-talk shows that it becomes loudest in two types of social context. It is prominent where the state apparatus denies to all or some of its citizens those freedoms which are truly basic to human functioning, when the needs and desires of the individual are subordinated to a centrally determined 'collective' purpose. And, paradoxically, it also becomes prominent in libertarian societies where an individualistic ethos assumes the good of all to be simply the sum of the good of each, so that 'free choices' and rights to them become invested with value in themselves. Rights claims of this second sort, moreover, seem the more persuasive when they are put forward at a time when many societies are entering a period of liberalisation, and attempting to grant or reinstate rights of the first sort.

Whatever the context, though, the purpose of invoking rights in moral or political argument is to make a claim which gives special status to what is sought. This claim implies that whatever liberty or entitlement is so labelled should not be denied or overridden by the usual pragmatic considerations of the outcomes in general welfare terms of treating given individuals in particular ways. That is why it has been noted that in conflicts of interest between individuals and between groups within a society, 'rights' function like trumps in card games, overriding, or seeking to override, pre-existing priorities and pragmatic trade-offs. In an individualistic context, therefore, such trumping moves should be treated with caution, for unless the good of all *is* truly equivalent to the sum of the good of each (and this is highly debatable in the matter of the rights of individual parents to exercise consumer choice and control in education) those moves may result in further advantage for those already with winning hands.

Before this is elaborated, two particular confusions inherent in talk of rights must be clarified, the first being the confusion between moral claims and legal entitlements, the second being the elision of differing orders of rights. On the first matter, in stressing the controversiality of rights talk, the discussion here has been referring to those moral entitlements which are claimed to be owed to individuals, irrespective of current legislation in the societies to which they belong. For convenience, we can call these 'moral rights', acknowledging all the controversiality which attaches to debate about what *ought* to be the case and how people ought to be treated. However, statements about what *is* the case, and about how people are in fact treated, are much more straightforward, particularly when that treatment is specified in legislation. It is thus a straightforward matter to state what rights in law are held conventionally by members of a given society, for these are simply those freedoms and entitlements that are enshrined in legislation. We might argue about whether these conventional rights in law give adequate protection to the individual, or whether they deny adequate protection to the welfare of the group, but what 'conventional rights' exist at a given time and place is a factual matter. Confusion arises because it is not always clear, when emphatic pronouncements about rights are made, whether we are referring to moral rights (where emphasis is rhetorical and persuasive in intent), or to conventional rights (where emphasis is strictly factual). In saying, for example, that everyone has a right to freedom of speech, we might be advancing a moral claim whose truth is a matter for ethical debate, or be making a factual statement which can be checked against the social system under which that 'everyone' happens to live.

Although these two kinds of right – the moral and the conventional – are logically quite separate, discussion and polemic frequently appeal to one of them to substantiate claims for the other. If we make the moral claim, for instance, that everyone has a right to freedom of speech, we are not simply reporting a state of affairs, but tabling a demand that social arrangements be maintained or modified to secure legal and institutional endorsement for this somehow pre-conventional and extra-legal moral entitlement. In the same way, when it is asserted that parents have a right to make choices and exert influence over their children's schooling, then, in advance of relevant legislation, this is a persuasive demand, where the rights formulation seeks to trump pragmatic considerations about possible effects on other interested parties and on the system as a whole. Once relevant legislation has been enacted, as now in this case, the assertion becomes *conventionally* true. Whether this new conventional right should be welcomed without reserve remains an open question, however, and in examining it we should be alert to the fact that conventional rights, in turn, reinforce the moral claims which they endorse. For in labelling social arrangements 'rights' rather than simply, say, 'opportunities', we are not merely stating that certain courses of action are now possible. It is also implied that wise and responsible individuals will avail themselves of those new opportunities which are presented as redressing a prior, less morally satisfactory set of arrangements.

DIFFERING ORDERS OF RIGHTS

In examining how far the persuasive force of rights-talk should lead us to set aside pragmatic considerations of outcomes, we must also take care to clarify the second source of confusion, by distinguishing between differing orders of rights. Of course, no rights are absolute, and we can always imagine counter-claims which could justifiably override any particular right but, nevertheless, the sort of counter-claims required to override a right to life are of a quite different order from those which would suffice to override a right to six weeks' annual paid leave or, in our society, to free medical attention should it be needed. The first example here –

the right to life – is perhaps the most basic example of those general rights such as freedom of thought, speech, movement, enquiry and freedom from arbitrary interference, which have greatest force, since they protect those immunities a person requires in order to operate as a rational autonomous being. Were it the case that parents, prior to the granting of legal rights to choice and control in schooling, had been deprived of such general rights, on their own or their children's behalf, then the justification for newly granted rights in education would be of the strongest sort. However, if none of the options for choice violates a general right, then choice between those options cannot be necessary to securing a general right. Conversely, if any of the options does violate such rights, they have no place within a free society. The second example – the right to six weeks' leave – is a contractual or special right, which comes into being as a result of negotiation between parties presumed equal in a transaction. Such rights might arise between individuals during the educational process (through active participation of parents in school government, for example), but they cannot exist prior to the transactions from which they would derive. That leaves us with the remaining possible analogy with educational rights: the third example above – the right to free necessary medical attention – which is neither a general right, nor a contractual right, but rather a welfare right, arising from arrangements which individuals in a given society have collectively agreed for their mutual support and welfare. Being based on such contingent social agreements, welfare rights are socially relative, and are therefore more negotiable than general or contractual rights, which tend to lend them overmuch force by association.

Precisely because welfare *is* socially relative, welfare rights are claimed by individuals against other members of the same collective, and therefore they are only binding if certain conditions obtain. Broadly, individuals are entitled to claim such rights, (a) if without them they would suffer direct disbenefit in relation to other members of the collective, or (b) if their obtaining them, even though it gave them direct relative advantage, would also indirectly benefit the group as a whole. If, for example, we apply those ground rules to the matter of a right to education, it seems clear that in a society such as ours that right could be justifiably claimed on both grounds. For in a society in which some receive education and in which personal development and life chances depend partially on it, all individuals are entitled to demand access to that education without which they would be relatively disadvantaged – condition (a). And in so far as society as a whole benefits reciprocally from the education individuals receive – condition (b) – the welfare right to an education is doubly justified. However, this argument cannot simply be extended to a parent's right to choice and control in schooling, for it would be over hasty to treat all rights questions which arise *in connection with* education as if they were subspecies of educational rights; that is, rights *to* education. Rights to state funding for education with a religious foundation and for parental choice in this connection may well be claimed to raise fundamental rights issues, since certain non-secular world views might consider a secular education to be a contradiction in terms. This chapter does not address that particular issue, which would require analysis of some of the paradoxes of pluralism, but attends rather to schooling choices where options are not claimed to threaten basic rights to freedom of belief.

EDUCATION, SCHOOLING AND RIGHTS

If a parent required the right to choose or control a child's school because some current schools, out of which the parent wished to opt, were so poor that what they offered was tantamount to no education at all, then the right to choose or manage *would* be a subspecies of educational right. However, the demand ought then to be that these sub-standard options cease to fall to the lot of any individual, rather than that they remain as possibilities only for those children whose parents – for whatever reasons – failed to act as effective agents on their behalf in a competitive situation. If parents are to be regarded as the appropriate educational decision-makers, then in that case the demand should be, not for each parent individually to select or manage each child's school, but for parents to determine collectively what characteristics should be common to all schools, thus eliminating the differences in quality which would underpin this 'right to choice' in education. There is no space here to elaborate the point that to leave control of educational decisions to the government of the day cannot approximate to such a process in an adversarial political system.

If, on the other hand, we assume that all schools do meet some minimal criteria such that they are deemed to offer 'an education' – and there can be no other justification for any school's existence in a context of compulsion – then a parent's rights to choice and influence within existing educational options does not merit the status of a welfare right under condition (a). It might do so under condition (b), if it could be shown that, given these rights to choice and control, even though some parents will secure additional advantage for their children *within* the group, those who suffer thereby in relative terms will nonetheless gain in absolute terms. Put bluntly, this assumption depends on a faith in the benign workings of the market: on believing that though a hierarchy of quality between schools will be exacerbated, quality at the lower end will be greater than in a less differentiated system. Since this is an empirical question, to be settled after the event, it will be left aside here, although below, when we examine the two kinds of benefit which accrue to individuals from schooling, it will be shown that even if a benign market *did* deliver increased cognitive and cultural advantage to less privileged consumers of education, it would necessarily also deliver increased social and economic disadvantage to those same consumers.

If this can be adequately established, then the parents' rights at issue here are not straightforward welfare rights, but rather rights of choice, or consumer rights. And in spite of current fashion, 'rights to choose' have no axiomatic legitimacy, but depend upon further moral argument which takes account of our relation to the object of choice and of the effects of any choice on other parties. We have the right to choose to dye our teeth purple if we wish, not because we have a dental right, but because we have a property right over our own teeth; we have the right to choose to eat cheese rather than pudding, when what we eat concerns only ourselves. But we do not have the right to choose what side of the road we drive on, as that choice affects other road users. If, indeed, what recent legislation has given parents is the right to exercise consumer choice and influence in education, we will need to ask whether freedoms to exercise consumer choice in the schooling context are, in fact, private liberties whose exercise concerns only the chooser. Firstly, however, since the consumers involved are parents, it is necessary to look more closely at the justificatory basis of rights held on behalf of third parties, for the grounding of such rights is pertinent to throwing light on our central question.

TRUSTEESHIP, PROXY RIGHTS AND THE SCHOOLING CONTEXT

We must, therefore, before examining the mismatch which follows from applying a rights-based approach – with all its individualistic assumptions – to the arbitration of competing interests within a social sphere which is competitive in outcomes, turn to the question of the special difficulties which arise in questions of *parental* rights, in whatever context these are exercised. These difficulties remain even when legality and morality are properly distinguished, and even when we do not confuse the different levels of justificatory force of differing orders of rights.

For whereas rights are normally thought of as straightforwardly protecting the actual or putative interests of rights holders themselves, this is rarely so in the case of parents. For although it is sometimes argued that parents have rights over children which are designed to protect the parents' own interests (Bridges, 1984), that is seldom the primary focus of contemporary discussion. And even in questions of rights over children, the parents' interests as rights holders in relation to the child are less likely to be backed by claims that *their* interests and welfare are overriding, than by claims that the eventual welfare of *children* is also best served by protecting the present interests and wishes of their parents. That may either be on the grounds that there is an identity of interest between parent and child, or on the grounds that the parent is the person best placed and/or most strongly motivated to act as the child's trustee or agent until such time as the child becomes competent to choose and act autonomously. So, even when parents' rights are to be exercised *over* children, they make implicit reference to those children's present or future welfare and interests. This is even more obviously the case when the rights in question are proxy rights, exercised by parents on their children's behalf. Parental rights in such cases are unambiguously grounded in the parents' duties as trustees of their children's welfare and as agents for securing those children's interests. When proxy rights are at issue, we have to consider whether the chosen proxies are in fact those best placed to choose and act in the interests of the individuals they represent, thus the abilities of parents to discharge their duties as proxies are basic to justifying all third-party rights accorded to them. At first sight it seems obvious that the most suitable proxies for children must be those closest to and most concerned about them: their parents. This may, however, not be the case in some areas of life, since the ability of anyone to make wise choices depends not just on characteristics of the chooser, but also on features of the object of choice.

So what are the relevant features of education, the 'good' over which parents are now given the right to exercise choice and control, each as proxy for individual children? The complicating conundrum here is that education is a good which is *at the same time* both private and unlimited, and also social and logically rationed. This puzzling paradox needs brief elaboration. In its first aspect, in so far as any individual's experience of education develops them in cognitive, emotional and cultural ways, the growth and fulfilment of an individual neither threatens nor harms the similar growth of any other individual. But, in its social aspect, public education in a complex and open society does not just further the private development of the individual, acting as a source of intrinsic value for them. It is also the primary mechanism for dispensing public exchange value, with performance and its credentials serving as currency of different denominations which can be cashed for access to life-chances of differing desirability. In its exchange value aspect, therefore, there will always have to be educational winners and losers, even if all were winners on the intrinsic value aspect (which would assume not only a pedagogical millenium, but also suppose that exchange value outcomes have no motivational effects). This inescapable feature of public education in modern, developed societies has been well summed up by noting that educational attainments are like numbered lithographs: their worth to those who have them depending in part on others lacking them (Hollis, 1982).

The upshot of these double, contradictory aspects to educational benefit is very significant to the justifiability of proxy consumer rights in education. In so far as education promotes the private development of the individual, then it seems clear that individuals or their proxies should have the right to exercise choice and control over their access to and experience of it, with a view to affecting outcomes for themselves. But in so far as it allocates differing life chances and their stratified rewards *between* individuals, so that the outcomes for each are enmeshed with the outcomes for all, a series of problems arise from an emphasis on individual rights in a context which is inescapably social. There are basically three kinds of problem arising: the first entails inevitable disbenefit to some of the pool of consumers; the second makes what counts as benefit problematic to all of the pool of consumers; the third results from the consequent curtailment of wider preferences in which the same consumers also have legitimate interests. We need now to examine each of these in turn.

INDIVIDUAL AND SOCIAL OUTCOMES: CONSEQUENT DILEMMAS

Little time is needed to describe the first and most obvious of these problems, which results from a combination of the logical point that, in exchange value terms, education necessarily must have losers as well as winners, coupled with the obvious fact that some children have parents who are more effective as agents than are others. In this case, to increase the rights of children's proxies is to ensure that winning or losing in the educational game is even less a result of characteristics inherent to the child than it has been up to now. The consequent ratcheting of the spiral of cumulative advantage and disadvantage which passes from one generation to the next would seem to be contra-indicated both by the moral claims of social justice, and by the economic claims of human capital theory.

The second problem is more complex, since it affects all parents acting as their children's trustees in a situation which has all the characteristics of a Prisoner's Dilemma. This is the kind of situation, first noted three thousand years ago, where individuals cannot achieve the best outcomes for themselves by pursuing their own interests directly and exclusively, but only by co-operating with other interested parties to modify the boundaries within which they make choices of available outcomes. Thus a market in education creates a competitive framework in which parents as consumers can seek relative advantage for their children. But it also creates a situation in which each child becomes vulnerable to the unspecifiable effects of the aggregate choices of other children's proxies. The libertarian assumption is that wise and effective parents will avail themselves, through their social purchasing power, of the opportunities made possible in that ᵣ ᵇᵉt. To suppose that this is the wisest move, however, is ᵣ overlook the changed parameters for choice which resuᴊ unspecifiable effects of aggregate choices, or endorsᵉ with them a set of value commitments which have loᵣ subject of political and moral debate.

It has already been pointed out that it is by no means obvious that the interests of children in general are best served by a ratcheting of the spiral of social competition, since some are bound to lose out. It should also be noted that it is perennially controversial, whether the interests even of those particular children who are likely to compete effectively are better served by securing additional personal advantage for them than by facilitating their eventual membership of a group with narrower educational (and hence social) differentials. Since these *are* matters of debate, the appropriateness of the parent as prime trustee is called into question, for the parent is hardly in a position to weigh these alternative notions of the child's eventual interest evenhandedly. Since parents are not in a position directly to affect the social situation, but only the position of their own children within it, they must, as trustees, adopt a conservative and prudential social stance, seeking the most advantageous outcome for their wards in the circumstances as currently given. In a context structured like a Prisoner's Dilemma, trustees have no responsible option but to make individualistic, competitive moves, even though these must entail a worse outcome for some of the young – and will certainly bring a changed (and debatably a worse) outcome for all of them – than would have resulted from a less competitive framework for decision.

Moreover, even if the broader and longer-term interests of children *were* beyond dispute, so that individual trustees did not have a hidden hand twisting their evaluative arms, there remains the further question of the rights of agency of parents in securing those interests. Where social goods are at stake, parents have no more rights to secure relative advantage on their children's behalf than any individual would have on his/her own behalf. In medical matters, for example, the rights of parents as sole agents for their children's welfare are granted only prima facie and can be overridden by the courts on the basis of both medical and moral argument. Where those medical matters concern not simply treatment of the child in question, but also imply concomitant changes in the treatment or resources for treatment available to other children, parents' rights of agency are not even granted prima facie.

In some matters, the conflict of interests which arises between individuals each exercising the same choice rights to their own advantage is self-resolving. For example, under British law parents have the right to give or withhold consent to medical treatment in the interests of their child, as in vaccination against infectious diseases. A parent who has good reason to suppose that a sufficient number of other parents will consent to that procedure, and who also knows that in rare cases it carries a serious risk, might rationally decide to withhold consent in the best interest of his/her own child. In doing so, however, that parent acts against the best interest of children in general, with the consent of the state whose duty is precisely to secure the interests which are thereby infringed. This conflict is self-limiting, however, for if more than a tiny minority of parents adopted the 'rational' strategy, it would cease to be rational. But apparently similar conflicts in the educational context are not self-limiting, being more like a parent's right to obtain for a child, with resources not shared by all, scarce medical treatment which cannot be made available to all. For if the exchange value of education, in combination with the stratified nature of the society in which it is embedded, make the relative advantage of one child in part a *necessary* function of the relative disadvantage of other children, then parents cannot seek to promote the interests of their own children without indirectly affecting the interests of other children. And the state cannot simultaneously discharge its duty to promote individual liberty *and* its duty of trusteeship for the young in general. Indeed, when the goods in question are positional, as education has been shown to be, far from being self-limiting, the dilemma is synergistic or self-exacerbating, with the momentum which is generated making choices progressively more stark.

This means that to grant rights of choice and control in education to parents may increase their freedom to make choices within immediate and short-term options – in this case of available educational experiences for their own children. At the same time, however, the exercising of this right forecloses on a range of broader and longer-term political choices, for the conflicts which arise between individual and collective outcomes are synergistic, and the effective individual chooser becomes, willy-nilly, one of the blind puppeteers of the 'hidden-hand' which operates the educational market. That market, in turn, will have considerable effects on the social situation for all of us in the future, and on the degree of diversity and stratification which individuals experience within it, producing orders of social change which previously were considered a fit subject for open political debate. Thus an increase in the individual's educational choices pre-empts a range of socio-political choices, so that rights to proxy consumer choice in education become not so much simple increases in personal liberty, axiomatically to be welcomed, as extensions of freedom in some areas of life, in exchange for diminutions of freedom in other areas – an exchange to be evaluated by weighing the relative costs and benefits of those losses and gains.

Since the social changes produced by the hidden hand of the educational market will be matters of degree, and since each individual, choosing separately, is unable to take the unforeseeable consequences of others' unknown choices into consideration, no individual chooser can determine the market outcomes which ensue, although each has a part in blindly producing them. In this way, we get the third of the problems noted here as arising from the granting of proxy consumer rights in education, for the opportunity to exercise choice over a broad range of socio-political preferences is thereby curtailed for the whole pool of consumers.

CONCLUSION

The analysis in this chapter has been unavoidably complex, for despite popular rhetoric, that is the nature of the issue in question. This volume looks at various aspects of the changing role of parents in the educational process. When the role of parents changes in matters which clearly affect them as trustees of their children's welfare and agents for securing their children's interests, two aspects to each issue must be kept in mind: how proposed changes directly affect the individual parents, and how they affect parents in general as a category of consumers and citizens. In this latter respect, the two kinds of value that education confers – intrinsic value and exchange value – and the twin functions of education – to develop the individual and to maintain and develop society – render the rights and roles of parents in the education process especially problematic. This chapter has focused on parents' rights in education, and particularly on their newly granted rights to increased choice and control over the education of their own children, revealing this addition to our armoury of personal liberties to be something of a double-edged sword.

This newly granted set of legal rights has been presented to the public as the overdue acknowledgement of proper moral claims for individuals (or their proxies) to exert control over important areas of their own life, rather than deferring to the arrangements of the state and its bureaucrats and professionals. As such, formulated in 'rights-talk', the changed arrangements for educational provision and the new opportunities offered to the individual seem axiomatically desirable, and proof against arguments which stem from fears for the less advantaged in the changed situation, and for the social (and political and economic) effects resulting from an educational system which evolves under market-driven pressures. It is not the job of an analysis like this one to arrive at evaluative conclusions about particular changes in educational policy; its purpose is rather to tease out hidden complexities, and to point out what questions those complexities raise.

Accordingly, this examination has shown that to formulate proposals for change in the language of rights and individual freedoms does not necessarily provide a knock-down case for those proposals. It has been shown that rights-talk is persuasive in intent and in effect, since we tend – mistakenly – to treat differing orders of rights as if they were equally morally binding. When educational rights were examined, it was argued that these were welfare rights, to be justifiably claimed and accorded if either or both of two conditions (representing relations between individual claimants and the group of individuals within and against which they are claimed) were satisfied. It was clear that, given the complex nature of education in our society, a right *to* education would be an essential personal liberty in that society. Matters became far less straightforward, however, when scrutiny moved on to rights *in* education, of choice and control. The complexities arising had two sources: the proxy status of rights holders, and the double-faceted nature both of the good over which rights are to be exercised and of the benefits to accrue from it not only to individual choosers but also to the category of choosers as a whole. This gave rise to three principal problems arising from the granting of the rights in question: inevitable disadvantages to an unspecifiable proportion of the pool of consumers; a problematising of what should count as benefit for consumers as a whole; and a curtailment of wider preferences which are also of consequence for that same pool of consumers. Each of those problems renders proxy rights a mechanism whereby individuals each have the opportunity, on behalf of their charges, of more control over their own moves in a competitive situation. Simultaneously, however, they raise the stakes for their own charges as well as others, with the unspecifiable outcomes of those raised stakes contributing to shape the context in which both proxies and direct consumers consequently pursue their lives and exercise their liberties. Given these complexities, whether or not the granting of proxy consumer rights to choice and control in education is on balance to be welcomed, regretted, or welcomed with qualification, is a matter for further moral and political debate and judgement. The purpose of this analysis has been to show that the granting of such rights is not a question axiomatically above debate.

REFERENCES

Bridges, D. (1984) 'Non-Paternalistic Arguments in Support of Parents' Rights', *Journal of Philosophy of Education* 18(1): 55–61.

Dworkin, R. (1977) *Taking Rights Seriously*, London: Duckworth.

Hollis, (1982) 'Education as a Positional Good', *Journal of Philosophy of Education* 16(2): 235–44.

The arguments of this chapter are further elaborated in two articles:

Jonathan, R. (1989) 'Choice and Control in Education: Parental Rights, Individual Liberties and Social Justice', *British Journal of Educational Studies* 37(4): 321–38.

Jonathan, R. (1990) 'State Education Service or Prisoner's Dilemma: The "Hidden-Hand" as Source of Education Policy', *British Journal of Educational Studies* 38(2): 116–32.

Chapter 3

Preconceptions about parents in education
Will Europe change us?

Alastair Macbeth

Education for a child is more than institutional provision. The relationship of parents to schools must be set in the broader context of parents' role in their child's total learning experience. Public pronouncements often equate education with schooling and unfortunately for some children it suits many adults to concur. Yet the goals of education, whether they be individual development, equality of opportunity, national prosperity, civic stability or any other, can only be approached if all the main educative forces are included. Schools alone cannot educate our children or solve our social problems. Perceptions about education precondition action, and a paradigm shift which recognises the impact of the family in general and parents in particular is, arguably, needed as a prelude to educational advance.

The family, however defined, remains the main unit of care for the child: a source of protection, nourishment, belonging *and education.* The quality of these attributes differs from family to family. The worst instances involve abuse, but such families are abnormal and most parents are genuinely concerned for their children's well-being, even if their efforts may sometimes be misplaced. Perhaps the essential point is that few people have thought of anything better than the family as prime unit for the bringing up (involving education) of children.

Government-funded, professionally staffed caring systems such as our medical, dental and schooling services do two things. First, they offer specialist facilities and expertise which most families cannot provide; that is, they supplement in-family care, even ensuring a safety-net on occasions when family effects are malign. Secondly, they can advise families on how they can help themselves, as with preventive medicine. They do not and cannot replace the family. Yet the rhetoric of education systems often seems to suggest that they can.

This can lead parents to think that they should 'leave it to the professionals' and 'not interfere', an attitude which may be reinforced by poverty and adverse physical conditions. However, we have ample evidence of correlation between home background and children's in-school attainment. Although we have yet to disentangle the relative effects of physical and educative forces in the home, we know enough to recognise that home-learning is a powerful factor both before and after schooling has commenced. The obvious professional response should be to harness that force, in the same way that a dentist urges daily tooth-care in the home. Yet as teachers we get and give little encouragement to do so.

School-learning and home-learning are supplemented by transmissions to the child, for good or ill, from wider society both through the media (especially television) and through the local community, including the peer group. Whatever television, newspapers and books a child encounters are much influenced by parents who also have some impact on where a child lives and with whom there is contact. Thus community-learning can be filtered by the family.

In considering the proper role of parents in their children's education, three commonly encountered assertions warrant consideration. They are:

- that children are not the property of parents
- that we should be concerned for the welfare of *all* children, not just individual children
- that schools should serve the function of helping children to grow away from dependence upon the family and to develop personal independence.

The obvious response to all three propositions is 'Yes, of course'. Where perceptions tend to differ is in what should be done about them and who should have responsibilities. In the 1960s and 1970s a view developed that schools could 'compensate' for family influence, despite the fact that more than eighty-five per cent of a child's waking (and therefore potentially learning) life from birth to sixteen is spent outside school, substantially in the family, and despite mounting research evidence of the educational influence of family and parents. Some authors recognised the impact of family but seemed to see parents and school as rivals, suggesting that 'the school may be seen not so much as the agent as the corrective of parents' (Musgrove, 1966: 136.) Fortunately, we are moving away from this view of the teacher as an *apparatchik* of the state to one in which parent and teacher can learn from each other. In their overlapping areas of activity each can reinforce the other's efforts for the benefit of the child with a recognition that the child is the property of neither state nor parent, though someone must have prime responsibility and the law places that responsibility on parents. Parents are therefore required to be agents for the child, but are helped and guided by professionals. In that capacity there is no legal requirement for parents to be involved in the education of other parents' children unless they are of that small minority of parents elected either to local government committees or to what in England are called governing bodies but which, with much the same functions, go by a host of names in other countries. And, of course, both parents and teachers can assist children to attain a sense of personal independence not just from the family nest, but also from all other childhood arrangements including schools.

The essential reasons for concentrating on the relationship of parents to schools are educational, and later in this chapter I shall outline five different paradigms of that educational relationship which may be encountered in Europe. First, however, I shall consider two politico-administrative issues. These are consumerism and parental representation in school management. Neither is educationally central but both are reasonable democratic facilities. The title of this book suggests that parents may be viewed as customers, managers or partners. Of course there is no reason why they should not be all three simultaneously and, indeed, other roles are possible. Meighan (1989) has offered six 'role definitions': parent as problem, as police, as para-professional aide, as partner, as pre-school educator and as prime educator. Munro (1991), studying both educational literature and political pronouncements, has developed a list of more than forty categories. I shall limit myself to the three in the title of this book, using the following sub-headings:

Consumerism
Parents in school management
Parents in education.

Each section will draw upon European examples and I shall conclude with some speculation about European influences in the future.

CONSUMERISM

There would appear to be a distinction in the field of education between consumerism and what might be termed 'clientism'. From one perspective the consumer of schooling is the pupil. Parents, as those entrusted by law with prime responsibility for the individual child's education, might be viewed as the school's legal clients. Yet the term 'consumerism' reflects an ideology by which market forces are brought to play in order to encourage competition from which, it is argued, efficiency of the institution increases. Baker (1988: 4) asserted of parental choice of school, 'This is an important end in itself. But at the same time it is a most powerful means of raising standards.'

Consumerism, although it champions individual freedom, has, as an additional objective, *organisational* change. By contrast, what I call clientism has *educational welfare of the individual child* as its main objective. There is overlap between consumerism and clientism in that both presuppose the right of the citizen to choose a service as a normal feature of a democracy. Two aspects of consumerism/clientism in education will be considered: parental choice of school and parental interest groups.

Parental choice of school

An educational argument for parental choice of school is that parental enthusiasm for an institution may improve pupil confidence in it and therefore motivation. However, the more prominent reasons are personal liberty for citizens and accountability of schools. Arguments against parental choice include fears of middle-class advantage, damage to unpopular schools in disadvantaged areas through loss of pupils, the re-emergence of a 'two-tier' system, and difficulties of forward planning for administrators. As with any politically contentious issue, arguments tend to get exaggerated and polarised. After open enrolment had been introduced in Scotland in 1981 marginal difficulties did appear but in some instances they were less acute than had been predicted (University of Glasgow, 1986). As Adler *et al.* (1989: 220) suggest, some claims of both supporters and critics of choice have been borne out, others have not.

Generally, European countries allow for parental preferences, but at the same time tend to ensure some conformity through

national curricular guidelines, inspection of schools and the training and appraisal of teachers. There are two main approaches to
parental choice of school: choice between state and independent
schools on the one hand, and choice between state schools on the
other. Historical circumstances have led to diversity of assumptions within each category. For instance, the virtual absorption of
church schools into our state system, but with the facility for
parents to choose, has been taken for granted in Britain for many
years; yet in France the retention of independent control by
Catholic schools and the right of parents to choose them became
one of the central political debates of the mid-1980s. As Glenn
(1989) argues in his survey of parental choice in six nations, the
issue is becoming less a matter of choice between a state pedagogy
and a church pedagogy and more a matter of individual preference for a particular institution. He argues that there is no
longer the strength of conviction that confessional schooling has a
socially divisive effect nor that religiously neutral public schooling
is necessarily destructive to faith.

In countries such as Italy and Britain independent schools are
not (or are minimally) state-funded and therefore become the
preserves of either wealthy or self-sacrificing families; by contrast,
in the Netherlands, where independent schools are fully state-
subsidised, any child can go to any school and two-thirds of Dutch
pupils attend independently controlled establishments, thereby
diminishing accusations of élitism. That system also enables
groups of parents to set up their own schools. The distinction has
been made (Tickell, 1980: 16) between 'weak' choice which is
between options prescribed by others and 'strong' choice, by
which the chooser determines the nature of the option. Denmark
has the most thorough-going arrangement for 'strong' parental
choice. To quote the Danish Ministry of Education (1991: 29):

> Private schools may be established by groups of parents who
> have special educational ideas or interests . . .
> All private schools are entitled to receive state-subsidies, cover-
> ing up to 85 per cent of their operational expenditure directly
> connected with instruction, and loans of favourable terms may
> be granted for the setting up of new schools provided certain
> requirements are fulfilled.

Those requirements include a standard of instruction comparable
to that in state schools, a minimum number of pupils, adequate

sanitation and being open to inspection. This has given rise to the 'Little Schools' movement and about eleven per cent of Danish pupils attend such establishments set up by parents or other groups.

The English grant-maintained school (Scottish self-governing school) system is a special variant with parents being able to initiate the extraction of a school from education authority control. It is a matter for opinion whether this represents genuine local democracy in action or is legalised hi-jacking, but it is unusual in that a bare majority of those voting in one generation of parents can determine the nature of local state provision available to subsequent generations of parents.

Choice between state schools may either be between *types* of schools or between individual schools. The German tripartite arrangement at secondary level which still applies in most provinces is an example of the first, since 'In general, parents have the right to choose the type of school ... not, however, a particular school' (Stroebel, 1986: 11). A similar but more complex arrangement may be found in Belgium where linguistic and denominational differences predominate.

Choice between individual state schools was introduced in Scotland in 1981 and in England and Wales in 1980 and 1988. The essential point is that parents have the right of choice unless there are legally based grounds for refusal. The Scottish 1981 Act, for example, lists eight grounds to deny parental wishes. In some countries the right of parents to choose a state school may be a matter for local discretion, as in Denmark.

There are therefore several variants on the theme of choice to which we may add the Assisted Places scheme in Britain, the concept of education vouchers (applied in parts of the USA), and a possibility in the future of parents partly teaching their children at home but opting them into local schools to cover those aspects which they cannot provide within the family. There is also the question of parental choice *within* as well as between schools. What elsewhere (Macbeth, 1989: 21, 92) I have called 'main determinant decisions' affecting a child's educational future should be subject to consultation with parents. These include decisions about subject options, remedial assistance, what public examinations to take, and so on. The Danish 1975 education law (Section 11.3), for example, requires parent–teacher–pupil consultation about subject options and streaming at age fourteen, but the final decision rests with parents. Another question is whether parental permission should always be a prerequisite if a child is to be included in an educational experiment. The concept of parental choice within schools perhaps deserves more attention.

Parental interest groups

Another feature of consumerism is growth of parental interest groups. In some countries the peripheral nature of Parent–Teacher Associations (PTAs) has resulted in parallel parental activist groups. From the Plowden Report (1967) onwards the PTA movement has met with criticism and it is not difficult to agree with Tomlinson's (1984: 87) assertion, 'Because the aims of PTAs are to encourage consensus and agreement between homes and schools, they rarely incorporate mechanisms for dealing with conflict. Thus, when the interests of parents and schools do not coincide, PTAs may be of little value.' In her study of British parental organisations, Nias (1981) draws the same conclusion and adds that many of the activities of such bodies do not appeal to parents.

There are dangers in generalising about other parts of Europe, but the tradition there has been more to have 'pure' parental organisations rather than confusing objectives by including teachers. Some of these are locally, regionally and nationally influential and in some cases (Germany, Norway, the French-speaking parts of Belgium) they have offices in government buildings. Ireland, which lacked a parental movement of any substance until the 1980s, has rejected the parent–teacher philosophy, and its new National Parents' Council has substantial state funding whilst retaining independence as an interest group with local- and school-level branches.

The European Parents' Association has encountered difficulty in accepting British parent–teacher organisations as members and has done so only reluctantly. It is my view that we need a distinct parental interest group movement at policy-making levels in the UK, while at the same time pursuing a philosophy of parent–teacher co-operation in the process of educating the individual child. A way forward (Macbeth, 1989) would be to have mini-PTAs, one for each class, but with parental organisations at school, education authority and national levels.

PARENTS IN SCHOOL MANAGEMENT

There is a conceptual linkage between parental interest groups and the election of parental representatives to boards of school management. Assuming that parent members are elected to governing bodies and similar organisations in order to represent those who elected them (a view which is not always adopted), then it is quite logical for parental organisations to be involved in that election process. In some German provinces the parents' council chooses representatives on the *Schulkonferenz*, while the recent Portuguese law (Portugal, 1991) makes it a requirement that parent members of each school's board are elected through that school's parent association.

Democratic theory recognises different kinds of representation, the extremes being trustee representation (by which the people elected act according to conscience without any further reference back to those who elected them) and delegate status (in which they constantly do so). Between these are various shades of compromise. Part of the argument for trustee status is that at national level and, to some degree, at local government level it is difficult for representatives genuinely to ascertain and reflect the views of their constituents. At the level of the school that argument applies less, especially if there is a parental interest group which can provide a network of contact with grassroots opinion. Yet local democracy is not the only argument for parental representation on governing bodies and school boards. The educational welfare of children as a whole and accountability for the efficient management of the school may be seen as other overarching purposes, a topic which I have discussed in greater detail elsewhere (Macbeth, 1990, chapter 2).

There is substantial variation throughout Europe in the extent of parental representation on such boards and the powers which parent representatives wield. Denmark and Scotland are atypical in having a voting majority of parents, whilst in other countries there may be equal numbers of parents and teachers (e.g. Dutch primary schools and schools in parts of Germany). In some (e.g. Italy, France) parents and teachers may be balanced in numbers, but representation of other groups will ensure that no one category is in a majority. Elsewhere (e.g. England and Ireland) parents outnumber teachers, but are still in an overall minority, whilst in Spain and Portugal teachers outnumber parents.

Proportions of membership become significant if the powers of the board are substantial. There is much variation throughout Europe in the extent to which such councils control, advise or monitor the school or merely exchange information. There are some indications that while the systems established in the 1960s and 1970s are mostly advisory, the emphasis in the 1980s has been more upon the management of schools, with some systems (e.g. England) giving boards considerable control. Danish school boards are of particular interest in that, with their parent majorities, they have the power of *approval* of major policy proposals put up by the school's head: in effect the power of veto. The Scottish school boards legislation of 1988 is also exceptional in that it has built into it the potential for a board to bid for increased power when it feels ready to do so, though there has been little sign of boards utilising this facility. Indeed, much of the research into boards of participatory administration (Baron, 1981; Beattie, 1985; Macbeth *et al.*, 1980; Macbeth *et al.*, 1984) suggests that, in general, such bodies have been reluctant to challenge professional control and generally do not represent 'parent power'. In many instances, parents on such boards have been socialised into loyalty to the board rather than committed to a philosophy of representing parental interests, and some official training materials for board members, such as those for Scotland, have been reticent in giving guidance to parents about representation (O'Brien, 1991).

PARENTS IN EDUCATION

Consumerism and parental representation in school management, defensible though they may be in terms of local democracy and a free society, are peripheral to the focal business of educating the individual child. There seems to be some confusion about what should be the proper relationship of parents to schools. That confusion, to a degree, stems from the fallacy touched upon at the start of this chapter that education can be equated with schooling.

In order to confront this dilemma, surely we must turn attention to that substantial proportion of a child's learning which happens outside school remorselessly, unavoidably, often randomly and messily, often deliberately and effectively, sometimes beneficially and sometimes not. Much out-of-school learning happens in the home, especially in the early years, and some of it is deliberate teaching by parents. Parents also have influence on the sorts of media, community and peer-group which the child encounters. The process and its relationship to schooling are complex and, as yet, incompletely researched or understood (Marjoribanks, 1979; Mortimore and Blackstone, 1982; Tizard and Hughes, 1984) but it seems clear that home-learning, reinforced by consistency of contact and natural bonding, has a powerful influence, especially on attitudes which are learnt. Further, it is clear from research stretching back to the 1950s that there is a linkage between a child's home background and in-school attainment, a process in which parental encouragement and home teaching play a marked part.

Thus it is not just that parents are legally responsible for their child's education and that parents provide much of it themselves, but what they provide influences and perhaps sometimes determines the effectiveness of teachers in schools. To portray graphically the relative influence of educative forces on a child is impossible, but a crude stylised model may assist in breaking away from the persistent implication in pronouncements by politicians, administrators, teachers and others that education is the same thing as schooling (see Figure 3.1).The image lacks statistical basis, except in one respect. The proportion of a child's waking life from

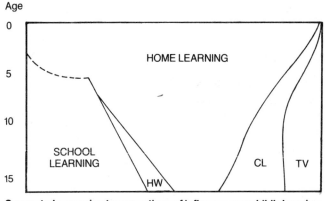

Suggested approximate proportions of influence on a child's learning

HW = homework set by school CL = community learning
TV = television + media

Figure 3.1 Model of influences on a child's learning

birth to sixteen spent in school is less than fifteen per cent. However, this chart embodies the assumption that school's *influence* is greater than fifteen per cent because it is professionally provided and the school element has therefore been magnified visually. In reality, proportions of each element will vary from child to child. With the crude indicator of this model in mind, and with a recognition that community and the media also have impact, we may turn to preconceptions about the relative contributions of home-learning and schooling to a child's education. Five stages in a continuum are considered in turn:

Education as home-learning only
Education as home-learning augmented by schooling
Education as both home-learning and schooling
Education as schooling augmented by home-learning
Education as schooling only.

Education as home-learning only

In most European countries, including Britain, there is no legal requirement for parents to send their child to school. The 1937 Constitution of Ireland, for instance, having placed responsibility for education on the family, states, 'Parents shall be free to provide this education in their homes.' In Britain we are more oblique, using the terms 'or otherwise' (Education Act 1944, Section 36) and 'or by other means' (Education (Scotland) Act 1980, Section 30). The number of families pursuing home education is not known. Meighan (1989) reports that UK subscribers to 'Education Otherwise', the mutual support organisation for home educators deriving from John Holt's philosophy, is over two thousand, while others opt for the more formal 'World-wide Education Service' which has been recognised by the Department of Education and Science (DES). It is uncertain how many subscribers use these materials to supplement rather than to replace schooling, or how many families educate their children at home without these aids. Lines (1987: 510) says of the USA, 'The actual number of children in home instruction seems to have grown from about 15,000 in the early Seventies to well over 120,000 today – perhaps as many as 260,000.' However, as she points out, this is less than one per cent of the total school-age population. Reasons for home education have been researched by Williams *et al.* (1984) and they conclude that, in general, home educators 'appear to be succeeding both in terms of their own purposes and expectations and in terms of traditional measures of success'. My own subjective observations of home-educating families in Strathclyde Region support this conclusion, and I have been impressed by the commitment of these practitioners.

The central point for this chapter is that it is possible to hold the view that schooling may be irrelevant to education *in practice*. The darker side of the picture, however, concerns families which neglect education or neglect their children. Of the five finalists for the 1991 Alcuin Award (given by the European Parents' Association and the European Commission for exceptional parent-involved educational initiatives) two were rectifying family deficiencies of educational provision, one concerned with the 'travelling people' of Ireland and the other with street urchins in Portugal. Williams *et al.* recognised this problem, but reported that in their American research 'we have encountered only one or two of these cases. It appears that generally home schooling parents are extremely conscientious'.

Education as home-learning augmented by schooling

I have encountered one family which has successfully negotiated with its education authority the facility for its children to take part in those aspects of schooling which, for reasons of equipment or expertise, it cannot provide at home. A more common mode is to alternate between spells of full-time schooling and full-time opting out, which, as Meighan (1989) reports, can be infuriating to the authorities. Other forms of *flexi-schooling* are possible. For instance, home educators can combine into school-like groups for parts of the week, and the Human Scale Education Movement, launched in Oxford in 1987, encourages the growth of small schools and the facility to opt in.

Yet the philosophy need not be small scale or informal. A vivid demonstration of this is the Italian parental organisation *Famiglia e Scuola* (FAES: Family and School). On the one hand it offers family training programmes and on the other it owns and manages fourteen schools. By any measures the FAES schools which I have visited are highly professional institutions, but quality teaching, important though that may be, is not the point. These schools are designed *to supplement home-learning*. Couples, not just mothers, commit themselves to a process of educating their children with the school assisting. They attend inter-family discussions and belong to the 'Department of Family Co-operation' in their efforts to improve what they provide for their children at home.

Inevitably this demands a high level of commitment by parents and an observer quickly notes that participating families are generally middle-class and Catholic, but the *concept* can be extracted from this particular social setting. Both parents and teachers commit themselves to a Charter of Educational Principles which includes the statement: 'Parents are the first and most important educators of their children.'

Education as both home-learning and schooling

This is the middle position. It recognises (in addition to the efforts of community and the media) two main *loci* of children's learning: the home and the school, different in structure and process but of equal educational status. There has been much use of the word 'partnership' between parents and teachers, but quite trivial and subservient parental actions may be paraded as educational partnership. However, serious authors have considered a genuine participatory approach (Widlake, 1986; Wolfendale, 1989), and Bastiani (1987: 104) has referred to a new ideology which 'stresses the complementary nature of parent and teacher roles, the need to recognise important differences between them and to confirm parental strengths, in a spirit of co-operation'. Since John Bastiani is contributing a chapter to this book, I shall leave this topic to him.

An alternative approach to education as partnership deserves mention. I call it the 'separate arenas' approach. This would accept that in-school and out-of-school educational actions can be developed in isolation from each other. Schools would be left to concentrate on a limited role – largely the transmission of specified knowledge and skills, plus a contribution to guidance – and to do it professionally. Schools would no longer have to pretend that they are attempting to 'educate the whole child'. Meanwhile, the Department for Education (DFE) (in Scotland, the Scottish Office Education Department (SOED)) and the education authorities might recognise that they would have wider responsibilities than would schools. Through enhanced use of the media, parental advisory centres (outside schools), home-learning specialists and other professionals, they could mount a campaign to alert parents to their unavoidable educational impact and provide guidance about home-educating to reinforce the work of the school. The Inspectorate's remit would also expand from being inspectors of schools to being inspectors of education. However, these steps would be costly and would insufficiently utilise teachers as agents in the process.

Some might want to go further and change the law to make teachers primarily responsible for the in-school education of the individual child, leaving parents responsible for attendance and out-of-school education. We know that such a change in the law would be workable because it would simply confirm the way that many parents and teachers behave today. But it would pose three problems. First it would fly against international declarations that parents should have prime responsibility for their child's education. Secondly, it would not fully overcome the problem that how children achieve in school is related to what parents think, say and do at home which, in turn, requires knowledge by parents about their child's schooling. Thirdly, by reducing parental duties, it would also reduce the facility currently available to schools to expect co-operation from parents. At the end of this chapter I return to the question of parents' obligations.

Thus the separate arenas approach, although attractive in some respects, runs the danger of sacrificing a vital relationship between parent and teacher. Partnership seems a more hopeful route, though perhaps supported by media publicity and by increased involvement by other professional groups.

Education as schooling augmented by home-learning

This is comparable to the approach labelled (though not advocated as ideal) by both Widlake (1986) and Bastiani (1987) as the 'communications' model. It assumes that home-learning should be an adjunct to schooling and that all is well if parents can understand and support what the school is attempting to do. Many schools in Europe have been adopting this philosophy.

Some initiatives have been a question of schools improving previous facilities, such as school brochures, report forms and parents' nights. Thus the revolution in desk-top publishing has improved presentation of school publications, though content continues to be criticised (Atherton, 1982; Bastiani, 1978; Jowett and Baginsky, 1991; University of Glasgow, 1986). School report forms have started to include spaces for parents to respond and the SOED has included that element in an official proposal (Scottish Office Education Department, 1991). Parents' nights are gradually shifting away from ignominious cattle markets and privacy is sometimes achieved. As Goacher and Reid (1985) point out, report writing is time consuming and the same may be said for consultations if they are really to be planning sessions. Several authors (Jowett and Baginsky, 1991; Macbeth, 1989; Tizard *et al.*, 1988) have referred to the under-resourcing of links with parents. Perhaps teachers' conditions of service will have to be changed and staffing levels altered. We probably need to go beyond the position in Denmark where 250 hours a year of every teacher's time is allocated to non-teaching tasks, prominent among which is co-operation with parents. We may agree with the Danish Teachers' Union (1991: 39) that 'home–school cooperation of today is so vital for the school that we must find the resources which are necessary to make that cooperation work.'

The National Foundation for Educational Research (NFER) study of parental involvement in schools (Jowett and Baginsky, 1991) offers depressing reading. In a section on meetings for parents the authors state, 'The few parents who attended would have gained very little and may indeed have felt reluctant . . . to attend future events' (p. 48). However, one of the simplest and most time-economic modes of educational contact between parents and their children's teacher(s) is one which has blossomed in parts of the Continent but is appearing only tentatively in Britain. This is the class meeting. Different types of class meeting are found throughout Europe, but the Scandinavian model is perhaps the most fruitful since parents have status, are involved in planning the meetings, and are encouraged and assisted through them to help their children educationally at home. I have discussed the issue more fully elsewhere (Macbeth, 1989, Chapter 6), but what is relevant here is the recognition that all parents with children in the same class have the learning experience of that class in common and see the meeting as affecting their child. Parents are therefore more likely to attend and to respond in their home-based teaching.

It is also from Scandinavia that a more worrying philosophy is emerging which, since it may be used to defend traditional teacher-centred attitudes, warrants exposure. The analogy is made with airlines. Airlines tend to distinguish between *main aims*, especially to transport a group of people safely from A to B, and *subsidiary aims,* especially personal service through peripheral facilities such as comfortable waiting areas and in-flight meals. Teachers seeking to perpetuate the school-centred view of education argue that what parents should be given is a pleasant entrance hall to the school, a welcoming atmosphere and the verbal equivalent of a sedating in-flight cocktail. A welcoming atmosphere is to be applauded, but this analogy, like many such comparisons, is inappropriate. Passengers are not expected to help fly the airliner. By contrast parents should and unavoidably do contribute to their child's education.

Education as schooling only

In practice this category cannot exist except, perhaps, in certain kinds of orphanage, since education inevitably happens outside school. Unfortunately, pronouncements by politicians and others often imply that when they use the term 'education' they are referring to institutional provision.

EUROPEAN INFLUENCES IN THE FUTURE

The Single European Act, passed in 1986 to take effect on 1 January 1993, is largely economic and on the surface has little to do with education. Indeed, like the original Treaty of Rome itself from 1957 it does not cover education, though it does mention training. However, it is difficult to separate economic from educational issues and the European Parliament and Commission are already active in the educational field with a range of programmes. The founding father of the European Community (EC), Jean Monnet, is reported to have said (it is often quoted) 'If I had to do it again I would start with education'; and a statement by the Commission of the European Communities (1988, Supplement: 1) to the Education Council asserted 'Education and training are . . . at the very heart of European construction.' The Director of the EC Task Force on Human Resources, Education, Training and Youth has referred to 'the trend towards integrating education and training' (Jones, 1990: 1). The Treaty on European Union (the 'Maastricht Treaty'), (Council of the European Communities 1992) goes further by giving education and training separate articles; that for education (Title II, article 126) stating, 'The

Community shall contribute to the development of quality education by encouraging cooperation between Member States and, if necessary, by supporting and supplementing their action', followed by specified areas of action.

It may be noted that the EC can affect education without passing educational laws. America provides a model by which the federal government influences èducational provision in the states which are responsible for education. There are two main methods. One is by funding educational initiatives and the other is through civil rights. We may discern something of the same approach in Europe. That the EC has been financing initiatives in the educational field in support of its own priorities is evidenced by the programmes which have emerged such as LINGUA (language teaching), PETRA (initial vocational training), Youth for Europe and others.

With regard to rights, we may expect impact from the Commission's concerns with equality of opportunity, education of migrant workers' children, free movement of persons, mutual recognition of qualifications, consumer protection, health and safety and other topics. Bids for charters of rights are emerging. A recent example is the draft report of the European Parliament's committee which deals with education (Gröner, 1991) about the problems of children. It calls for twenty-eight actions, among them a 'legally binding European Charter of Children's Rights' (p. 6).

With regard to parents the EC's initial interest seems to have been consumerist. The Commission has backed the European Parents' Association (EPA), having held a conference in Luxembourg based on the Glasgow University report which first recommended the creation of EPA and having supported it since. At the time of writing, EPA itself is debating a possible parents' charter. What is unusual and, in my view, encouraging is that it aims to be a charter not just of rights but also of duties of parents. While its current draft embodies rights for parents to raise and educate their child, to have access to schooling, to 'continuous care for the quality of education by the responsible public authorities', to information, to choice of school and to be consulted about policy, it counterbalances these demands with duties on parents to raise children in a responsible way, to 'commit themselves personally to the school education their children receive', to be well informed, to encourage respect for other people's convictions, and to ensure that they, as parents, are represented.

Such a charter brings us back to the fundamental question of how the contribution of parents to their child's education is perceived. The five categories of preconception discussed above are attitudinal. Attitudes are a preparedness to act and they are learnt. From the Plowden Report (1967) onwards there has been interest in the effects of parents' attitudes, but less focus upon the attitudes of politicians, administrators, inspectors and teachers. That may be changing. Jowett and Baginsky (1991) refer to the 'underlying attitudes' of staff in schools (p. 141) and the need for 'an explicit philosophy' (p. 143). It is just possible that a philosophy – or, more likely, several philosophies – might emerge from Europe to help us to achieve a much-needed paradigm shift for the benefit of children.

If so, I hope that such a shift will not just recognise the educational importance of parents and the inability of schools to counteract educational disadvantage without the support of parents, but may also put new emphasis, in a benign and understanding way, upon the obligations of parents. The concept of a school-and-parent contract which I first advanced in a report to the EC in 1984 and adapted into a less rigid 'signed understanding' (Macbeth, 1989, Chapter 2) is now being pursued by others in different forms (Labour Party, 1990; National Association of Head Teachers, 1988) and the EC has contributed to a project on the topic by the Royal Society of Arts (RSA) (Jones *et al.* 1992). All these schemes, including my own, have tended to convey the assumption that education is schooling augmented by home learning, with quite modest commitments by parents to the formal teaching process. That, of course, does not preclude much more substantial parental contributions unconnected to institutional provision. In the long run we may hope that some form of partnership between parents and teachers, but with recognition that other agencies have a part to play, will become the norm.

Initially, closer links with other European countries will highlight the existing diversity of practice. I would expect that gradually, through funding and civil rights issues as well as some growing consensus based on awareness of good practice, pressures will mount for greater homogeneity in education, including the part played by parents in it.

REFERENCES

Adler, M., Petch, A. and Tweedie, J. (1989) *Parental Choice and Educational Policy*, Edinburgh: Edinburgh University Press.

Atherton, G. (1982) *The Book of the School*, Glasgow: Scottish Consumer Council.

Baker, K. (1988) 'English Educational Reform', Baron, G. (ed.) (1981) *The Politics of School Government*, Oxford: Pergamon. Brussells: *EPA-INFO* 3: 4–5.

Bastiani, J. (ed.) (1987) *Parents and Teachers 1: Perspectives on Home–School Relations*, Windsor: NFER-Nelson.

Bastiani, J. (ed.) (1988) *Parents and Teachers 2: From Policy to Practice*, Windsor: NFER-Nelson.

Beattie, N. (1985) *Professional Parents: Parent Participation in Four Western European Countries*, Lewes: Falmer.

Commission of the European Communities (1988) Statement to the Education Council, Brussels, 24 May, quoted in *Eurydice Info* no. 5, June 1988.

Council of the European Communities and Commission of the European Communities (1992) *Treaty on European Union*, Brussels: EC.

Danish Teachers' Union (1991) *Teachers' Union Journal*, 28 February.

Education Act 1944, London: HMSO.

Education Reform Act 1988, c. 40, London: HMSO.

Education (Scotland) Act 1980, c. 44, Edinburgh: HMSO.

Education (Scotland) Act 1981, c. 58, Edinburgh: HMSO.

Glenn, C.L. (1989) *Choice of School in Six Nations*, Washington, DC: US Department of Education.

Goacher, B. and Reid, M.I. (1985) *School Reports to Parents*, Windsor: NFER-Nelson.

Gröner, L. (1991) Draft report of the Committee on Youth, Culture, Education, the Media and Sport, 19 June, European Parliament.

Jones, G., Bastiani, J., Bell, G. and Chapman, C. (1992) *A Willing Partnership*, London: RSA/NAHT.

Jones, H.C. (1990) 'Education and Training', *Eurydice Info CEDEFOP News* (December).

Jowett, S. and Baginsky, M. (1991) *Building Bridges: Parental Involvement in Schools*, Windsor: NFER-Nelson.

Labour Party (1990) *Parents in Partnership*, London: Labour Party.

Lines, P.M. (1987) *An Overview of Home Instruction*, Phi Delta Kappa.

Macbeth, A.M. (1989) *Involving Parents: Effective Parent–Teacher Relations*, Oxford: Heinemann Educational.

Macbeth, A.M. (1990) *School Boards: From Purpose to Practice*, Edinburgh: Scottish Academic Press.

Macbeth, A.M., Corner, T., Nisbet, S., Nisbet, A., Ryan, D. and Strachan, D. (1984) *The Child Between: A Report on School–Family Relations in the Countries of the European Commission*, Brussels: EEC.

Macbeth, A.M., Mackenzie, M.L. and Breckenridge, I. (1980) *Scottish School Councils: Policy-Making, Participation or Irrelevance?* Scottish Education Department, Edinburgh: HMSO.

Majoribanks, K. (1979) *Families and Their Learning Environments: An Empirical Analysis*, London: Routledge & Kegan Paul.

Meighan, R. (1989) 'The Parents and the Schools – Alternative Role Definitions', *Educational Review* 41(2): 105–12.

Ministry of Education (1991) *The Education System*, Copenhagen: Ministry of Education.

Mortimore, J. and Blackstone, T. (1982) *Disadvantage and Education: DHSS Studies in Deprivation and Disadvantage*, London: DHSS Heinemann Educational.

Munro, C. (1991) personal communication related to Ph.D. studies, University of Glasgow.

Musgrove, F. (1966) *The Family, Education and Society*, London: Routledge & Kegan Paul.

National Association of Head Teachers (1988 and 1990) *The Home–School Contract of Partnership (A discussion paper)*, Haywards Heath: National Association of Head Teachers.

Nias, J. (1981) 'Parent Associations', in Elliott, J., Bridges, D., Ebbutt, D., Gibson,R. and Nias, J. *School Accountability*, London: Grant McIntyre.

O'Brien, J.P. (1991) 'A Study of the Scottish Office Training Programme for School boards', M.Ed. thesis, University of Glasgow.

Plowden Report (1967) *Children and their Primary Schools*, Department of Education and Science, London: HMSO.

Portugal (1991) *Decreti-Lei 177/91*, 10 May, on School Councils.

Scottish Office Education Department (1991) *Reporting 5-14* (Working Paper No. 14), Edinburgh: HMSO.

Stroebel, H. (1986) 'Choice of Schools in the Federal Republic of Germany (with Special Reference to Bavaria)', paper for meeting of national representatives and experts on Evaluation and Monitoring of the School System, 15–17 September.

Tickell, G. (1980) *Choice in Education*, Canberra: Australian Schools Commission.

Tizard, B. and Hughes, M. (1984) *Young Children Learning, Talking and Thinking at Home and at School*, London: Fontana.

Tizard, B., Blatchford, P., Burke, J., Farquhar, C. and Plewis, I. (1988) *Young Children at School in the Inner City*, London: Lawrence Erlbaum.

Tomlinson, S. (1984) *Home and School in Multicultural Britain, Education in a Multicultural Society*, London: Batsford.

University of Glasgow (1986) *Parental Choice of School in Scotland*, Glasgow: Parental Choice Project, Department of Education, University of Glasgow.

Widlake, P. (1986) *Reducing Educational Disadvantage*, Milton Keynes: Open University Press.

Williams, D.D., Arnoldsen, L.M. and Reynolds, P. (1984) 'Understanding Home Education: Case Studies of Home Schools', paper for American Educational Research Association, New Orleans.

Wolfendale, S. (ed.) (1989) *Parental Involvement: Developing Networks between School, Home and Community*, London: Cassell.

Chapter 4

Parental choice and the enhancement of children's interests

Michael Adler

I have suggested elsewhere (Adler, 1990: 70) that the changes brought about by the parental choice provisions in the 1980 Education Act and the 1981 Education (Scotland) Act (which were inserted into the 1980 Education (Scotland) Act) can be interpreted in a number of ways:

• As a shift away from an authority-wide approach to school admissions (which enables education authorities to prevent overcrowding and under-enrolment, deploy resources in an efficient manner and pursue their own conception of social justice) towards a parent-centred approach (in which parents decide what is best for their children and parents' concerns have priority over those of the education authorities).

• More generally, as a shift away from a collective-welfare orientation (which focuses on the achievement of collective ends, is primarily concerned with the overall pattern of decision-making, develops rules and procedures to achieve the programme's ends, and recognises the necessity for trade-offs between the various ends the policy is trying to achieve) towards an individual-client orientation (which focuses on each individual case, respects individual autonomy and assumes that individuals are capable of deciding and acting for themselves, allows individuals to challenge unfavourable decisions and precludes the possibility of trade-offs).

• As the first step of a two-part deregulation of the educational system in which market-like relationships between schools and parents replace bureaucratic and political forms of accountability. In this two-stage process, the first stage comprised the introduction of parental choice while the second stage involved the delegation of powers and responsibilities from education authorities to individual schools and a greater involvement of parents in their management.

Prior to 1988, deregulation had proceeded further in Scotland than in England and Wales. This is because the parental choice provisions in the 1981 Education (Scotland) Act were considerably stronger than the analagous provisions in the 1980 Education Act, and Scottish education authorities had much weaker powers to control school admissions than local education authorities in England and Wales. Under both pieces of legislation, parents were given a statutory right to request the school they wished their children to attend, the circumstances in which authorities could reject parents' requests were restricted, and parents were given the right of appeal to a specially constituted appeal committee. However, the two pieces of legislation differed in three important respects:

- While the statutory exceptions to the authority's duty to comply were broad and general in the English legislation, they were much more specific in the Scottish legislation. The primary exception in England, which applied (under Section 6(3) of the 1980 Education Act) when compliance 'would prejudice the provision of efficient education or the efficient use of resources', enabled an authority to justify a refusal by referring to conditions in schools other than the one requested by the parents. By contrast, the primary exceptions in Scotland, which applied (under Section 28A(3)(a) of the 1980 Education (Scotland) Act) when compliance would either entail the appointment of an extra teacher or significant extensions or alterations to the school or 'be likely to be seriously detrimental to the order or discipline of the school or to the educational well-being of the pupils there', meant that the authority could only refer to conditions at the school requested by the parents.
- Whereas in England the decision of the appeal committee was final, in Scotland parents could appeal against an adverse appeal committee decision to the courts. This not only gave parents a second chance to appeal but also allowed appeals to be heard by a sheriff, whose civil jurisdiction is roughly equivalent to that of an English county court judge, who is clearly independent of the local authority and less likely than an appeal committee to be predisposed in favour of its concerns.

• When an appeal is upheld in Scotland, either by an appeal committee or a sheriff, the authority is required to review the cases of all parents in similar circumstances who have not appealed and, if its decisions are unchanged, it must grant the parents a further right of appeal. There were no analagous provisions in the English legislation (Adler 1990: 69).

It is true that stronger demand-side deregulation in Scotland was partially offset by a greater degree of supply-side deregulation in England and Wales. Thus, school governing bodies in England and Wales had somewhat greater powers than Schools Councils in Scotland but this was of little significance since neither was in any position to mount a serious challenge to the centralised decision-making powers of the local authority.

The position in England and Wales was completely changed by the provisions of the 1988 Education Reform Act. In relation to parental choice, the Act strengthened the rights of parents and reduced the powers of local education authorities, introducing a form of 'open enrolment' similar to what Scotland has had since the early 1980s. Local education authorities were prohibited from setting maximum admission limits below the physical capacity of the school and from refusing to admit children when there was room for them at the schools. Section 26(1) of the Act equates 'physical capacity' with the 'standard number' and stipulates that 'the authority . . . shall not fix as the number of pupils in any relevant age group it intends to admit to the school in any school year less than the relevant standard number' which is defined (under Section 27(1)) as either the number of pupils admitted to the school in 1979, when school rolls were substantially higher than they were a decade later, or the number admitted in the previous year whichever is the greater.

In relation to the local management of schools, the 1988 Education Reform Act introduced a degree of delegated financial management which is substantially greater than that envisaged even under the 'ceiling' provisions of the 1988 School Boards (Scotland) Act. Thus, in England and Wales, the governing bodies of all secondary schools and primary schools with more than two hundred pupils now receive budgets from the local authority which they are free to spend as they wish. The budget covers the vast majority of schools' running costs, including staff salaries. School governors can decide what to spend the budget on, that is how much should go on teachers' salaries and how much, say, on support staff or school equipment. Schools are expected to operate rather as though they are small businesses: their income depends, to a very large extent, on their success in attracting pupils since about seventy per cent of the local authority's education budget is distributed to schools by means of a formula (which must be approved by the Secretary of State) in which a minimum of seventy-five per cent is in direct proportion to pupil numbers, weighted by age (Lee, 1990). By contrast, schools do not control their own budgets in Scotland and school boards only have limited powers (Munn, 1991). These include taking part in the appointment of senior staff, approving the headteacher's plans for buying books and materials and receiving and making representation on reports from the headteacher and the education authority. Under the 1988 School Boards (Scotland) Act, school boards can ask to be given further powers, for example to decide which children can enter the school, to determine what is taught in the school and to 'hire and fire' staff, but none has actually done so.

Considering these two sets of developments together, it is clear that demand-side deregulation in England and Wales has caught up with its earlier development in Scotland while supply-side deregulation has been taken a good deal further. The 'uncoupling' of schools from local authorities and the replacement of bureaucratic and political forms of accountability by market-like relationships between parents and schools has been taken a stage further in England and Wales than it has in Scotland. How long this disparity will be allowed to continue, particularly following the 1992 election victory for the Conservatives, is a matter for conjecture.

THE IMPACT OF PARENTAL CHOICE IN SCOTLAND

In an attempt to assess the significance of the parental choice provisions introduced into Scotland by the 1981 Education (Scotland) Act, Alison Petch, Jack Tweedie and I carried out a programme of research into the origins, implementation and impact of the legislation. Our research was carried out between 1983 and 1986 and reported on in a recently published book (Adler *et al.*, 1989). Our main findings were as follows:

- Across Scotland, about ten per cent of parents have made a 'placing request' for their child, at entry to primary school and at transfer to secondary school. (The latest available figures (Scottish Office Education Department, 1991) indicate that 14.2 per cent of the parents of children in Primary 1 (P1) and 11.1 per cent of the parents of children in Secondary 1 (S1) made a placing request in 1989/90.) However, in the cities, the proportion has been much higher (twenty to twenty-five per cent) and, in some city areas, it has been more than fifty per cent.

- These requests have come from right across the social class spectrum. However, although there was no overall relationship between social class and parental choice, there were often strong relationships at the local (school) level. Whether or not this has led to increased social segregation is an important question, although it is not one which we were in a position to answer.

- Avoidance of the district school was important for a majority of parents who made a placing request in each of our case-study areas. For the one hundred and fifty parents of P1 children in our sample who made a placing request, avoidance of the district school was important for sixty per cent (range fifty-four to seventy-eight per cent in three case-study areas); for the two hundred and ninety parents of S1 children in our sample who made a placing request, it was important for sixty-nine per cent (range sixty-one to eighty-one per cent in four case-study areas).

- For a majority of these parents, choice involved finding a satisfactory alternative to the district school rather than making an optimal choice from a wide range of possible schools. At S1, sixty-two per cent of those who made (or considered making) a placing request considered only one alternative to the district school while twenty-seven per cent considered two alternatives. At P1, the tendency was even more marked; seventy-nine per cent considered only one alternative and a further seventeen per cent chose two.

- In requesting schools for their children, parents were influenced much more by geographical and social factors, for example proximity and discipline, and by the general reputation of the school, than by educational considerations, for example the curriculum, teaching methods or examination results. They relied on rather limited and second-hand information about the schools concerned.

- Most requests (about ninety-three per cent) have been granted either initially or on appeal. However, there has been a significant drop (from ninety-six per cent in 1982/3 to eighty-nine per cent in 1989/90) in the number of successful requests for secondary schools as authorities have closed annexes, removed temporary accommodation and imposed intake limits to prevent overcrowding (Scottish Office Education Department, 1991).

- Appeal committees have tended to uphold the authorities while the courts have, on the whole, upheld the parents. This is not altogether surprising. Appeal committees contain a majority of councillors and members receive little or no training. The courts always prefer to individualise disputes – thus most sheriffs have focused on the single child who is the subject of the appeal rather than the intake limits set by the authority. Since it is very difficult to argue that the admission of one more child would have any significant effect on a school, most sheriffs have decided in favour of parents. It is fortunate for the authorities that few parents have appealed to the sheriff; in one authority, where there have been a substantial number of appeals, the authority routinely concedes the case at this point.

- Because of declining school rolls and because most intake limits have not been challenged in the courts, few schools have really been overcrowded. However, some of them are certainly full to capacity, while a rather larger number of schools are chronically undersubscribed. Some secondary schools in urban areas now have first-year intakes of substantially less than one hundred pupils. In 1985, two out of twenty non-denominational secondaries in one city we studied and two out of ten in another had first-year intakes of less than one hundred; by 1988, the number of such schools had risen to eight.

- On the whole, the schools that have gained most pupils have been the formerly selective schools in middle-class areas. In contrast the schools that have lost most pupils have been those that serve local authority housing schemes in deprived peripheral areas. The effects of these movements on aggregate attainment levels and on the distribution of attainment between schools and pupils remain to be seen, but could well be quite substantial.

- There was considerable evidence of 'band-wagon' effects, and little evidence of the market functioning as a self-correcting mechanism. This is presumably because schools with diminishing rolls lose resources and parental support and frequently experience a fall in morale, all of which make it more difficult for them to attract additional pupils. The continuing decline in school age population has meant that few schools have actually been overcrowded.

These outcomes have given rise to a very inefficient use of resources since, other things being equal, expenditure per pupil is much higher in a school with a small roll than a school with a large one (Audit Commission, 1986). There have also been widening inequalities between schools since, even without formula funding, schools which lose pupils also lose staff and resources and can no longer offer comparable educational opportunities. The result of aggregating individual choices that may themselves be rational is a situation that many people would describe as irrational (Hirsch, 1977; Schelling, 1978). Perhaps more importantly, the threat to equality of educational opportunity has potentially very serious implications for a democratic society. In Scotland it has already led to the re-emergence of a two-tier system of secondary schooling in the big cities. This is different from the old, two-tier system which existed prior to the introduction of comprehensive schooling in that the lower tier now caters for a minority of working-class children whereas before it catered for the majority. However, the existence of a small rump of what are, in effect, junior secondary (secondary modern) schools located in the most deprived areas of the big cities is surely a cause of concern. What will happen when school rolls start to increase (as they will in a few years' time) and the second stage of deregulation starts to take effect (in England and Wales if not for the moment in Scotland) remains to be seen.

Although there have clearly been gainers as well as losers from the Scottish legislation, the balance sheet suggests that it has not achieved an optimum balance between the rights of parents (to choose schools for their children) and the duties of education authorities (to promote the education of all the children for whom they have responsibility). Although some children may have gained from the legislation, it would seem that they have gained at the expense of others and that those who have lost are those who could least afford to do so.

PARENTAL CHOICE AND SOCIAL JUSTICE

There would seem to be a prima facie case for arguing that the parental choice provisions in the 1981 Education (Scotland) Act offend not once but twice against John Rawls' second principle of justice for institutions. According to Rawls (1971: 302), justice requires that social and economic inequalities should be arranged so that they are both:

(a) to the greatest benefit of the least advantaged, consistent with the just savings principle and
(b) attached to offices and positions open to all under conditions of fair equality of opportunity.

The just savings principle refers to the sacrifices which people in one generation may make in order to secure advantages for those, including the least advantaged, in subsequent generations. One would need to have a great deal of faith in the 'trickle-down' effects of market forces in order to justify the educational disadvantages which the legislation has imposed on the most deprived children in the most deprived areas of society in order to satisfy the first condition. In any case, as Jonathan (1989: 333) has pointed out,

> Unless it is argued that ability and talent standardly correlate with parental agent-effectiveness (i.e. parental choice) then the predictable allocation of prizes in the market-competitive education game must represent a regrettable waste of human capital.

Since children's access to schools is mediated through their parents, and some parents will actively seek to promote their children's interests while others are indifferent towards them, it cannot be argued, from the standpoint of children, that schools are open to all under conditions of fair equality of opportunity. Thus, the parental choice provisions in the legislation do not appear to satisfy the second condition either.

It does not follow, or at least it should not follow from anything I have written so far, that a 'rights strategy' should be abandoned and that parents should be deprived of their rights to choose, or at least, express a preference for the schools they wish their children to attend. I should add, in parentheses, that even if this were thought to be desirable in principle it would be extremely difficult to bring this about in practice. If I have understood her correctly, I part company at this point with Jonathan's otherwise admirable critique of recent changes in educational policy (Jonathan, 1990) in that she would appear to be prepared to do just that.

My own position is that parents do have a legitimate concern with their own children's education and that this does extend to choice of school, and indeed to choice of subject (and possibly even to choice of teacher) within the school. This is because schools are not and ought not to be identical in all respects, and because some children will be happier and perform better in some schools; other schools will be more congenial and more appropriate for other children. At the same time, education authorities do have a legitimate concern with the education of all children in the community.

GOOD SCHOOLING AS A SOCIAL RIGHT

As Brighouse and Tomlinson (1991: 3) emphasise in a recent Institute of Public Policy Research (IPPR) paper,

> it ought to be the entitlement of every child to attend a 'successful school'.

They go on to argue that this necessarily demands some fettering of the application of market principles to the provision of education since these principles produce 'losers' as well as 'winners'. However, this situation undermines the basis of citizenship. They argue:

> To accept such a state of affairs in the design of provision and management of schools is to accept that some of our future citizens, through no fault of their own, are doomed to receive education in schools known to be 'failing'.

Like Brighouse and Tomlinson, I would also argue that every child ought to attend a 'successful' school and that market principles cannot be applied to education because they would result in some children going to schools which are clearly 'unsuccessful'. However, it is important to emphasise that there is no agreement, and probably never will be any agreement, as to what constitutes a 'good' or 'successful' school. This is because 'good schooling' and 'successful schooling' are 'essentially contested concepts' (Dworkin, 1986: 70–2) – there exist a number of coherent, plausible, and attractive conceptions of the 'good' or 'successful' school, each of which rests on different sets of value assumptions. The publication of 'league tables' comparing the examination results of pupils in secondary schools, such as those released just before the election by the then Scottish Education Minister (Fraser, 1992), and even the development of more sophisticated measures of the 'added value' which can be attributed to the school (McPherson, 1992) convey the impression that schools can be ranked in terms of a single criterion. Schools can, of course, be ranked on other criteria and, in terms of this particular criterion, schools with the same score (on either scale) may have little in common with each other. In any case, different pupils respond to different schools in different ways – thus, those school characteristics which are conducive to a particular conception of 'success' for one child may be quite different from those which are conducive to the same conception of 'success' for another child.

A BETTER BALANCE BETWEEN INDIVIDUAL AND COLLECTIVE CONCERNS: FOUR PROPOSALS

It is my contention that, in the recent past, many authorities were not sufficiently sensitive to parental concerns, but that, in attempting to redress this imbalance, legislation has placed too much emphasis on parental choice, and that this has, in turn, led to the re-emergence of unacceptable educational inequalities. Thus, the correct balance between individual rights and social justice, and between parental choice and equality of educational opportunity has still to be found. In the remainder of this chapter I propose to indicate how I think a better balance could be struck.

Encouraging diversity

As a prerequisite, I think it will be important to abandon the fiction that all primary and (comprehensive) secondary schools provide an identical set of educational opportunities and the aspiration that they should strive to do so. The common core curriculum (whether introduced on a consensual basis as in Scotland or imposed, by statute, as in England and Wales) provides the key to this. Over and above the common core curriculum, schools should be encouraged to develop particular curricular strengths, for example in music, the arts, sports, modern languages or technology. Education authorities could play a very important role here, similar to that played by the Universities Funding Council (UFC) in relation to universities, in the allocation of minority subjects to particular schools. In addition to developing particular curricular strengths, schools should also be encouraged to advance their own particular teaching styles, institutional ethos and extra-curricular activities. Of course, schools already differ in all these respects: what I am advocating is that they should be far more explicit about these differences than they currently are. Some schools might emphasise progressive child-centred learning while others stressed traditional didactic teaching; some might draw attention to their orderly, structured and disciplined atmosphere while others referred to their encouraging, non-authoritarian and tolerant characteristics; and different schools would highlight particular after-school activities, school exchanges and trips and competitive sports fixtures which they were particularly keen to promote. These different school characteristics would reflect, in part, the views of school boards and school governing bodies and, in part, those of the headteacher and the teaching staff, but education authorities would have an important role to play in preventing all schools from adopting a common set of characteristics and in ensuring an appropriate degree of diversity.

Abolishing catchment areas

In order to ensure the widest possible access to a range of schools with different characteristics, all artificial barriers to school admissions should be abandoned. I am referring here, in particular, to school catchment areas. Although open enrolment implies that parents may send their child to any school, almost ninety per cent of children in Scotland (and, one may assume, a similar proportion in England and Wales) still attend the school serving the catchment area in which they live. This is because most education authorities still use catchment areas and because parents are required to take the initiative if they do not want their child to attend the catchment area school. In towns and cities, it is rarely the case that school catchment areas represent local communities or neighbourhoods and more common for them to reflect administrative boundaries that have little salience for the population. Where they do represent local communities or neighbourhoods, they constitute the major source of inequality in educational attainment at school level and thus the major obstacle to equality of status and parity of esteem between schools. Of course, if children are to be really free to attend schools outside their neighbourhoods, free travel will probably have to be provided.

Promoting children's interests

Much more thought needs to be given to the interests which the right of school choice is trying to protect. At present, the legislation seeks only to protect parents' interests in choice. Since, as Jonathan (1989) points out very clearly, parents act as agents of their children but are not all equally effective in this regard, we need to consider children's interests directly. As schools already differ in many ways and would differ even more if my proposals were enacted, this would entail efforts to ensure that children attend those schools which are best suited to their particular personalities and talents. Teachers and parents will often have different views as to what these are: it is therefore important to find some means of involving them both in decision-making. In another recent IPPR paper, Miliband (1991: 20) refers to the need to emphasise co-operation rather than competition.

> It is the rules governing choice/preference that tilt the balance towards competition or co-operation but no system can eradicate either of them. The trick is to promote collaboration at all levels: between pupils, between parents and teachers and between teachers and LEAs.

If all schools were required to produce genuinely informative prospectuses; if parents and pupils were encouraged to visit all the schools concerned (rather than discouraged as is often the case at present); and if discussions were to take place between teachers, parents and, in the case of older pupils, the pupils themselves, this would enable teachers, parents and pupils to examine each other's reasoning, to decide what the child's interests were and how they could best be furthered. Miliband continues.

> Education and public services require a far more interactive relationship between client and provider. Parental input to school choice, often assumed to be inimical to a co-operative school system, can help match children to schools . . . Involving parents in choosing schools can be the first step towards a more productive relationship between school and parent for the rest of the child's school career: education is, after all, a partnership.

It is worth mentioning in this context that, if norm-referencing, which is currently the dominant approach to testing in primary and secondary schools, were to be replaced by criterion-referencing, teachers could use children's test results to discuss their progress to date with their parents and to advise on what would best promote their progress in future.

Protecting vulnerable schools

A greater measure of protection needs to be given to schools which have lost pupils and to the pupils who attend these schools. Parental choice has produced a number of chronically under-subscribed schools (mainly in deprived urban areas) which cannot provide educational opportunities comparable to those provided by other schools. However, in a democratic society, it is widely regarded as unacceptable that some children, through no fault of their own, should have many fewer educational opportunities than others. One way of preventing this would be to enable education authorities to set limits on admissions of pupils to schools which have gained pupils where there are good reasons for so doing, even if school rolls are less than the physical capacity of the schools (as in Scotland) or the numbers admitted in 1979 when school rolls were at their peak (as in England and Wales). Our own research indicated that the imposition of admissions limits on the most popular schools in one of the cities we studied provided a measure of protection for less popular schools although these limits lacked statutory force (Adler *et al.*, 1989, Chapter 5).

Over and above that, I would wish to reactivate a set of proposals which Bondi and I put forward in an article on the problems created by falling primary school rolls (Adler and Bondi, 1988). These involve the (local) education authority in determining a set of general policies, for example in relation to minimum, optimum and maximum school sizes and facilities, appropriate ability, social or racial mixes for schools, and in deciding on the level of financial support available for *groups* of schools serving particular communities. The education authority would, in addition, be responsible for costing and identifying the advantages and disadvantages of different configurations of schooling for the area, as Strathclyde Region has recently done (Strathclyde Regional Council, 1986) and as Lothian Region is currently doing. However, the decision as to which configuration would be adopted would not be taken by the education authority (as was the case in Strathclyde and Lothian) but, rather, by the affected parties in the local community. In this way, within the budgetary limits and the policy constraints laid down by the education authority, local communities could decide which configuration of schooling they preferred. It would, however, be incumbent on the education authority to lay down the procedures which local communities would be required to follow in reaching a decision.

AN ALTERNATIVE APPROACH TO PARENTAL CHOICE

Taken together, the four proposals outlined above constitute an alternative approach to education policy which takes choice seriously but, by structuring choice differently and altering some aspects of the context in which choice takes place, attempts to avoid some of the most unacceptable consequences of parental choice as constituted by the 1981 Education (Scotland) Act and, in all probability, by the 1988 Education Reform Act. In particular, it seeks a means of promoting children's interests and rehabilitating some legitimate collective policy concerns which have been entirely subordinated to parental choice by the 1981 Act in Scotland and the 1988 Act in England and Wales.

Because the most unacceptable consequences of parental choice are to be found in large towns and cities, the proposals outlined above are likely to have their greatest impact there. However, that is a strength rather than a weakness. In any case, they are likely to have some impact on all schools, including rural schools and schools serving sparsely populated areas where parental choice is of little significance. Such schools would be enjoined to eschew monolithic characteristics and to avoid competing with each other on a single set of criteria. They could, in fact, be encouraged to assume some of the characteristics of the 'omnibus school', first advocated as a model for secondary education by the Advisory Council on Education in 1947 (McPherson and Raab, 1988). Just as the omnibus school would have catered for all (academic and non-academic) pupils from a given area, albeit in rather different ways, so schools serving large areas could be encouraged to develop a number of different teaching styles and curricular programmes for children who would derive particular benefits from them. Such schools would attempt to provide a diversity of provision under one roof which compares with that offered by a number of different schools in an urban area. The modern department store which sub-lets floor space to a variety of retailers provides a model for such a school.

RESPONSES TO CRITICISM

The proposals outlined above have been criticised from many quarters. One set of critics is concerned that the core curricula for pupils aged between five and fourteen in Scotland and in England

and Wales are so congested that schools are in no position to develop particular curricular strengths. However, the existence of specialist music schools, denominational schools and City Technology Colleges, as well as the very considerable *de facto* variations in the curricular offerings of primary as well as secondary schools suggest that this criticism is not a particularly strong one. To the extent that the existing national curriculum is felt to impose too much of a straitjacket on individual schools, it would be appropriate to relax it somewhat.

A second set of critics has pointed out that, although different teachers adopt different teaching styles, teachers in a given school are likely to adopt a range of approaches to classroom teaching. This is particularly so in secondary schools where different departments may teach their subjects in different ways. Thus, even if it were possible to produce a robust characterisation of teaching styles it is inappropriate according to these critics to refer to a school's teaching style. Although I do concede that there is some force to this criticism, I think it is overstated. While it is clear that matching can never be an exact science, choices that are informed by some familiarity with the modes of teaching which the child is likely to encounter (along with other aspects of the school) should help parents and teachers make more informed choices which better promote the interests of the child.

A third set of critics has pointed out that the suggestion that schools might adopt different teaching styles has implications for assessment and would only be feasible if there were corresponding changes in the examination system. This is clearly correct and the two sets of changes would have to proceed hand in hand. However, it is worth noting that the development of 'criterion referencing' and the increasing use of school-based assessment (until government called a halt to these developments) suggest that the examination system is capable of taking on board a wider range of teaching styles than are presently to be found in order to do justice to pupils who learn best and have been taught in different ways.

A fourth set of critics has argued that attendance at a primary school with a particular curricular emphasis might disadvantage a child when it comes to choosing a secondary school. However, the fact that parents and teachers would jointly aim to match a child having a given set of aptitudes and abilities with a school that was conducive to that particular child suggests that this criticism is not a particularly strong one.

A fifth set of critics has suggested that we lack the knowledge to match children with schools and has expressed concern that the process would inevitably come to depend on intelligence and personality tests of dubious validity. While I am certainly not of the view that matching could ever be an exact science and would be vigorously opposed to the use of any tests other than the criterion-based tests that would be supported by the large majority of teachers, I cannot accept that education is, or ought to be, any different from several other areas of professional activity, for example medicine, social work and criminal justice, in which what is known as 'differential diagnosis and treatment' is applied. In any case, if matching were to be seen as an ongoing process rather than a once-and-for-all event (or, at best, two such events, one for primary school and the other for secondary school) and became part of an annual pupil appraisal, the risk of 'failure' would be greatly reduced as there would be repeated opportunities to correct 'mistakes' when these became apparent.

A sixth set of critics point out that parents and teachers would not necessarily agree on what was best for the child. This is obviously true – parents and teachers do not always agree now in their assessment of the children's ability or potential or over issues like subject choice or examination presentations. However, this objection should not be overstated since many parents and teachers reach agreement now and more could be expected to reach agreement after a full discussion. And, where they fail to agree, then subject to the availability of a place, the parent's view would still prevail much as it does today.

CONCLUSION

Liberal economic theory assumes that individuals are the best judges of what is in their own best interests. Whether or not this is true, it is fairly clear that parents are not necessarily the best judges of what is in their children's best interests. However, this situation is not one which parents can themselves remedy. The problem is structural rather than motivational. Institutional changes which would enable parents, with the assistance of teachers, to make more informed choices about the types of school which would best promote their children's learning and thus further their children's interests and which would re-emphasise some of the legitimate collective policy concerns which have been eclipsed by the construction of a 'quasi market' in education (Glennerster, 1991; Le Grand, 1991) need to be introduced. It would be fanciful to suggest that the task is going to be easy, but it would similarly be defeatist to conclude that, because it is clearly going to be difficult, it should not be attempted.

REFERENCES

Adler, M. (1990) 'Rights as Trumps: The Case of Parental Choice of School in Scotland', *Education and the Law* 2(2): 67–72.

Adler, M. and Bondi, L. (1988) 'Delegation and Community Participation: An Alternative Approach to the Problems Created by Falling School Rools', in Bondi, L. and Matthews, M. (eds) *Education and Society: Studies in the Politics, Geography and Sociology of Education*, London: Routledge.

Adler, M., Petch, A. and Tweedie, J. (1989) *Parental Choice and Educational Policy*, Edinburgh: Edinburgh University Press.

Audit Commission (1986) *Towards Better Management of Secondary Education*, London: HMSO.

Brighouse, T. and Tomlinson, J. (1991) *Successful Schools* (Education and Training Paper No. 4), London: Institute for Public Policy Research.

Dworkin, R. (1986) *Law's Empire*, London: Fontana.

Education Act 1980, London: HMSO.

Education Reform Act 1988, London: HMSO.

Education (Scotland) Act 1980, Edinburgh: HMSO.

Education (Scotland) Act 1981, Edinburgh: HMSO.

Fraser, D. (1992) 'A Hidden Agenda behind the Exam Tables', *Scotsman*, 4 March.

Glennerster, H. (1991) 'Quasi Markets for Education?' *Economic Journal* 101 (September): 1268–76.

Hirsch, F. (1977) *Social Limits to Growth*, London and Henley: Routledge & Kegan Paul.

Jonathan, R. (1989) 'Choice and Control in Education: Parental Rights and Social Justice', *British Journal of Educational Studies* 37(4): 321–38.

Jonathan, R. (1990) 'State Education Service or Prisoner's Dilemma: The "Hidden Hand" as Source of Education Policy', *British Journal of Educational Studies* 38(2): 116–32.

Le Grand, J. (1991) 'Quasi Markets in Social Policy', *Economic Journal* 101 (September): 1256–67.

Lee, T. (1990) *Carving Out the Cash for Schools: LMS and the New ERA of Education* (Bath Social Policy Papers No. 17), Bath: Centre for the Analysis of Social Policy, University of Bath.

McPherson, A. (1992) *Measuring Added Value in Schools* (Briefing No. 1), London: National Commission on Education.

McPherson, A. and Raab, C. (1988) *Governing Education: A Sociology of Policy Since 1945*, Edinburgh: Edinburgh University Press.

Miliband, D. (1991) *Markets, Choice and Educational Reform* (Education and Training Paper No. 3), London: Institute for Public Policy Research.

Munn, P. (1991) 'School Boards, Accountability and Control', *British Journal of Educational Studies* 39(2): 173–89.

Rawls, J. (1971) *A Theory of Justice*, Oxford: Clarendon Press.

Schelling, T. (1978) *Micromotives and Macrobehaviour*, New York: Norton.

School Boards (Scotland) Act 1988, Edinburgh: HMSO.

Scottish Office Education Department (1991) 'Placing Requests in Education Authority Schools', *Statistical Bulletin* no. 2/B6/1991, Edinburgh.

Strathclyde Regional Council (1986) *Adapting to Change* (Report of the Working Group on the Implications of Falling School Rolls), Glasgow: Strathclyde Regional Council.

Chapter 5

Parents as school governors

Michael Golby

The first generation of school governors constituted in maintained schools in England and Wales under the terms of the 1986 Education (No. 2) Act completed its first four-year period of office in 1992. Among these three hundred thousand school governors were about seventy-five thousand parent governors. Thus those four years saw the entry on the educational stage of a new force of people in a renewed institution of school governorship. Both private and maintained schools have always had a local overseeing body of some kind. In the public sector primary school 'managers' and secondary school 'governors' were largely decorative by-standers to the functioning of the system until the 1980 Education Act (which required that every school should have its own individual governing body to include elected parents and teachers), the 1986 Education (No. 2) Act (which increased the representation of parents and extended governors' powers over the curriculum and conduct of the school), and the 1988 Education Reform Act (which greatly increased the responsibilities of governors in the local management of schools). Traditional ceremonial governorship with its vague and impotent spectatorship to the work of local education authorities (LEAs) and the teaching profession is now well and truly superseded.

But what new settlement is to be found between the new school governing bodies and the other interests within the system, the LEAs, the teachers and central government? Is there room for the expanded powers of the new school governors in an educational system noted for its many interests, all claiming their own autonomy over areas of decision-making? What will be the internal relationships on governing bodies between parents, teachers and others? Above all, will better schools result?

PARENTAL INVOLVEMENT

Parents are involved in the new school governing bodies as elected members, in every respect equal to all other members. But of course parental involvement in schools is no new thing. From at least the time of Plowden onwards parental involvement has been a standard and dominant part of the rhetoric (if not always of the reality) of those professionals considering themselves progressive. Parental involvement has taken a number of forms but the focus has been on individual parents' responsibility for their own children. Parental involvement has been essentially the activity of private citizens seeking their family advantage. Parents relate to the school as private persons attempting to secure the best for their own children in a value system – that of the school – which is taken for granted on both sides. The middle classes, it is commonly argued, have been conspicuously successful in these processes since their own values, to some extent the product of their own successful schooling, have enabled them to understand and empathise with the culture of the teaching profession.

Only exceptionally have parents individually or collectively entered into a dialogue of equals about the general policy and practices of schools. Doing so is to enter into a public and social world and to consider policy and practice as it affects not only their own children but children in general. It is a change in focus from the private to the common good. This is the prospect that now faces school governors.

Governors must now ensure that the curriculum is broad and balanced and meets the requirements of the national curriculum; that courses leading to public examinations are for approved qualifications and follow approved syllabuses; that the law on religious education is complied with; and that information on the curriculum and pupils' achievements are communicated to parents. They must decide whether sex education should be provided and advise on appropriate content. They may offer the headteacher general principles on discipline. They take a part in selecting and appointing staff, including the headteacher, and in salary decisions. They must make statutory information available to parents, including the provision of an annual report to parents and the holding of an annual parents' meeting. They control admissions to the school. They control budgets, decide on staffing levels and on recruitment and promotion of teachers. They can also decide that a parental ballot to take the school out of LEA control should be held.

PARTNERSHIP

Those are the new obligations of governors, and they are a great leap beyond the traditional notion of partnership, between parents and school at local level, between teachers, LEAs and central government elsewhere. For partnership, traditionally, has been in the nature of a working understanding in which the various parties have evolved their own relationships as a matter of practice rather than principle. Partnership has not been underpinned by an explicit specification of the rights and duties of the partners. For example, in regard to school managers (the pre-1980 term for primary school governors) and governors, the Model Articles which followed the 1944 Education Act gave broad terms for local arrangements. Managers and governors were given care of the school premises, a share in budgeting for the school and appointing the headteacher and 'the general direction of the conduct and curriculum of the school'. In practice these powers were little exercised and the post-war curriculum became a professional secret garden until the 'great debate' of 1976–7 which set in motion the processes towards today's national curriculum. There was no partnership over the curriculum, its structure and assessment though there was, of course, considerable and growing involvement of parents at school level in helping their own children through a set of processes decided professionally. Partnership has been largely an honorific term referring to private not public activity, means rather than ends.

Partnership implies something of value contributed on a basis of equality from each towards the achievement of a common goal. Parental involvement has amounted to little more than a self-seeking acquiescence in disparities of power. Through the 1970s and beyond we see measures to stipulate the balance of power and to set up a legalistic basis for the rights and duties of the partners. Thus the Taylor Report of 1977, *A New Partnership for Our Schools*, asserted that there ought to be no area of a school's life which was not properly the concern of its governors.

We think of the governing body as a partnership bringing together all the parties concerned with the school's success so they can discuss, debate and justify the matters which any of them seeks to implement.

(Taylor Report 1977: 52)

The Green Paper, *Parental Influence at School* (Department of Education and Science, 1984), proposed that parents should elect from among their number a majority of seats on governing bodies. But this was rejected by organised parents' groups and by the National Association of Governors and Managers (NAGM). The Green Paper was probably the high-water mark of 'parent power', and its effect was to consolidate support behind the Taylor proposals for a quadripartite division of seats between parents, teachers, LEAs and members of the local community (Maclure, 1988: 131).

So long as partnership remained a matter of good practice rather than legal requirement it stood to veil inequalities of power under a gauze of good intentions. All too often it has served as a byword for acceptance of the *status quo*. Now we are inexorably moving to more legalistic and formal relationships in the education service, as elsewhere (Shearer, 1991). But what these new relationships are to look like in practice is still not clear, for they ultimately rely, not on the letter of the law, but upon the way in which the people involved conceptualise their situation. Since school governors are a new invention, albeit on a traditional base, we find a search for an appropriate metaphor going on. In new situations people decide how to act by asking themselves 'what is this really like' and it is not at all clear that a new idiom has established itself in such a way that governors know precisely what they are or should be doing. That is something which comes as a matter of practice.

We not only see but also behave in the way we do because, first and foremost, that is the way people see and behave in the tradition to which we belong.

(Langford, 1985: 20)

The problem for school governors is that there is as yet no tradition; the excitement of school governorship is that the tradition is in the making.

To understand what parents are doing as governors (and as a basis for arguing what they ought to be doing) it is necessary to interrogate what legally they ought to be doing and what in practice they actually do. This is a fundamental aim of this chapter. It will entail discussion of legislative intentions and a review of some research evidence as to governors' practice.

POWER: WINNERS *AND* WINNERS?

One theoretical point can perhaps be first established. It is sometimes said or thought that governors can only gain power at the expense of others, teachers perhaps especially, but also LEAs. School governors may alternatively be seen as adding power to the whole system, over against other competing social and political priorities, rather than causing a redistribution of a finite quantity of power within the education service.

Though there will be a realignment of practices – for example governors will consider the curriculum alongside teachers – the result may be greater power for both sides. Parents as winners does not entail teachers or others as losers. Also, and what is most important of all, the education service as a whole could be improved and empowered in its external competition for resources and esteem through the concerted efforts of the new partners in more equal and institutionalised relationships. Some measures, including particular forms of school governor training and support and the fostering of inter-school links, federations and the like, will be suggested below as ways in which the added value of parents as governors may make itself felt through the system as a whole.

LOCAL DEMOCRACY

A further and invaluable benefit looked for in the new arrangements for school governorship is in the general area of citizenship. A form of local participation in the welfare of the community through deliberation over the use of its common resources is offered to parents and others in the new arrangements. It is also a unique opportunity for there is no other institution so open to the involvement of the ordinary citizen as schools now are in England and Wales. In the areas of health and policing, for example, the lay involvement remains minimal and token. In schools, which lie advantageously at the heart of nearly every community, exists the opportunity for the development of an active citizenship beyond the assertion of purely sectional interests, for example that of the parents as (transient) consumers. Can the new school governors be seen as forerunners of a renewed democracy at the grassroots? Could it be that parent governors, emerging from the pursuit of private interests into the public realm, will provide new recruits to the active citizenry? If teachers are 'the forlorn hope of the culture of Western modernity' (MacIntyre, 1987: 16) perhaps some of the new governors will reinforce them.

GOVERNORS TODAY

Parents have attained a theoretical legitimacy in the running of schools, being represented in numbers equal to those of LEA nominees. Parents outnumber teacher governors (their numbers were increased in 1986 above the 1980 Education Act's provision while those of teacher governors were not). Parents are now in a position to participate in the running of schools as a potential major force alongside LEA nominees, teachers, co-opted governors and the headteacher if he or she elects to become a governor. (See Table 5.1.)

But how do these new governing bodies work in practice? What are the prospects for further development? How are parents to be supported in the push for participation? Are there limits to parents' participation as school governors? Are these limits different from those affecting other school governors?

PARENTS AS GOVERNORS

It is first necessary to consider the precise character of parents' situation as school governors since there are important ambiguities which come apparent with the practical implementation of the legislation. These stem from the political inevitability that legislation must appeal to a diversity of interests and motives if it is to reach the Statute Book in the first place. So what are parents supposed to be doing as school governors?

In the first place parents are equal members of the governing body and they share in the responsibilities of the whole body. It is important to notice that individual governors have no personal authority nor special duties except those that are properly delegated to them by the governors as a whole. In asserting the parental point of view, the stance of parent governors must be mediated by the governing body as a whole. As one among many,

Table 5.1 Composition of new governing bodies

For county, voluntary controlled and maintained special schools

Less than 100 pupils	2 parents 2 LEA-appointed 1 teacher 1 head (unless he or she chooses not to be a governor) *and either* 2 foundation governors (in the case of a voluntary school) and 1 co-opted member *or* 3 co-opted
100–299 pupils	3 parents 3 LEA-appointed 1 teacher 1 head (unless he or she chooses not to be a governor) *and either* 3 foundation governors and 1 co-opted *or* 4 co-opted
300–599 pupils	4 parents 4 LEA-appointed 2 teachers 1 head (unless he or she chooses not to be a governor) *and either* 4 foundation governors and 1 co-opted *or* 5 co-opted
More than 600 pupils	5 parents 5 LEA-appointed 2 teachers 1 head (unless he or she chooses not to be a governor) *and either* 4 foundation governors and 2 co-opted *or* 6 co-opted

Different rules apply to voluntary aided and special agreement schools
For such schools there must be:
   1 LEA-appointed
   1 (at least) parent
   1 or 2 teachers (depending on whether there are more or fewer than 300 pupils)
   1 head (unless he or she chooses not to be a governor)
plus enough foundation governors to ensure they outnumber the rest by two in a governing body of fewer than eighteen and three in the case of a larger body. One of the foundation governors must also be a parent. In the case of primary schools serving an area in which there is a minor local authority, the minor authority can appoint one governor.

a parent governor is responsible for the general conduct of the school as described above. But, as such, a parent governor has no special power or responsibility.

REPRESENTATION

Though parents as governors are equal with all other governors, they are elected by the parent body under specified procedures and are governors in virtue of their election. Thus they have a special relationship to the body of parents that elected them. They represent parents in the way teacher governors represent teachers. Parent governors and teacher governors are the only elected governors; LEAs, minor authorities and voluntary bodies nominate members; co-options may be voted upon by the governing body as a whole and headteachers may exercise *ex officio* membership.

The representative link between teacher and parent governors and their constituencies is the basis of their legitimacy. Yet there is no legal requirement on teacher and parent governors to report back to their separate constituencies; nor, for most parent governors especially, is there any obvious way in which they can systematically do so. Teacher governors have the advantage at least of a relatively small electorate and easy access to it. But parent governors are given no responsibility to work in any particular way among the parental body as a whole. So, with a few exceptions of the kind to be mentioned below, parent governors often find themselves elected but out of touch with their electors. Nor is this a one-way failure. Conducting an exit poll at an open evening in an Exeter middle school a researcher found that not a single parent could name any parent governor. Note the paradox here that attenders at a popular open evening, a successful event of the traditional partnership, could give no evidence of interest in parent governors. The explanation is not far to seek. Caring about your own child is one thing; entering into the public, social realm is another.

It seems then that parent governors will be governors first and parents second unless specific measures are taken to publicise their role. It will be another question how far this is desirable, of course. Are school governing bodies to be thought of as made up of separate, perhaps conflicting interests? Perhaps an element of this is necessary if governing bodies are not to 'co-opt' parents into a continued, mainly self-elected local élite. This was what Bacon (1978) found in an early study in Sheffield where elected parent governors (and student governors) had been introduced as a local initiative. The distaste for politics which parent governors often express and the belief that common sense and goodwill can prevail over ideology are poor omens for the quality of action and debate that may well be necessary in future if governorship becomes a disputatious affair.

If they are to represent the views of parents, and especially if they are not regarded, by themselves or others, as typical parents, parent governors must seek out such views. This touches upon the outside affiliations of governors, an under-researched area, because governors with strong connections to local networks will have better information than stay-at-homes. But to which networks and how representative will the knowledge that derives from them be?

Moreover, bringing to bear their understanding of parental opinion will present problems of assertion for some parent governors. They must assert themselves within their governing bodies and not all parents have the necessary skills. On the other side, procedural measures, such as appropriate chair skills, will be necessary to see that all governors' views are heard.

Parent governors are a unique category of parent by virtue of their performing a public service, presumably in some measure on behalf of other parents. Presumably they are to represent the parental interest, in so far as they can discern it, within the whole governing body and perhaps they are to be a special channel between the school itself and parents via the governing body. But how are such difficult duties to be fulfilled?

MODELS OF GOVERNORSHIP

We shall see that a proportion of parent governors admit to bewilderment in the face of their general responsibilities and their particular status as parent governors. There is a minority which feels marginalised by manipulative heads, outranked by LEA-nominated veterans, mystified by educational jargon, intimidated by paperwork (Golby, 1990). On the other hand there is another minority among governors which is entirely clear, perhaps all too clear, what it is to do.

GOVERNORS AS BOARDS OF DIRECTORS

Governors are to run the schools. A study of nine case-study schools found 'one in three governors representing almost all the schools likened the governing body to the board of directors of a limited company' (Baginsky *et al.*, 1991: 7) and observed that this view was particularly favoured by chairs and headteachers. 'Governors govern, heads manage' was the keynote for an Action for Governors' Information and Training (AGIT) seminar at the Department of Education and Science (DES) in mid-1991; it might have been added 'teachers deliver'. Part of what governors are exploring in practice is the boundary between governing and managing a school. Wilkins (1990: 5) defines governing as the 'establishment of policy and the monitoring and evaluation of that policy' and managing as 'translating broad policy into practice and establishing and maintaining appropriate structures and processes to ensure that policy objectives are achieved'. 'Running' schools lies ambiguously between these two broad functions. While, as Sallis (1991: 4) says, there is little evidence that governors want to run the schools they 'don't want it to be a game of pretend either'. What then is involved? What attributes need a governor possess? Deem *et al.* (1990: 7) believe that the distinction between governing and managing

> may be applied at two levels (at the level of beliefs and at the level of practical action) and hence may come to be interpreted differently by heads and governors.

They identify some governing bodies which make a sharp distinction between their role and that of the head and others which assert executive aspirations.

> This can lead to problems or at the very least to conflict and an overlap of responsibilities. Thus in the main study there is one school where a governor has worked out his school's budget on his home computer; we have also witnessed discussions in which governors have said to their headteacher . . . 'we run this school now and we decide what is to be done' even though they may find themselves unable to do so in the event.
>
> (p. 8)

In such a picture governors are seen as Boards of Directors. There is evidence that some governing bodies are establishing internal specialisms and often recruiting to them through the co-option process. The prime case following the devolution of budgets to schools has been the pursuit of the bank manager or accountant to deal with financial matters. Other skills in short supply, according to a survey of chairs were

> management and organisational skills; business and industrial skills. Some also mentioned marketing, legal, building, surveying and related skills.
>
> (Keys and Fernandes, 1990: 33)

Now, what is a parent, *qua* parent, actually to do on such an executive governing body? Leaving aside the contingency that a parent governor by chance possesses some professional or practical skills needed to run the school, what otherwise is a parent governor, as representative of parents in general, to do as a school governor? If the answer is that the parent governor is to advise the governing body of the likely reception among parents (consumers) for its decisions, a number of problems arise. What access has a parent governor to parental opinion? Many parent governors agonise about their relationship to their constituency. They nearly all differentiate between being a delegate and being a representative but many worry about the legitimacy of their position as representatives. Elections are often formalities, little contested. Annual Parents' Meetings are notoriously ill-attended events. Optimistic governors take the poor attendance to be a sign of satisfaction; pessimists take them to be another sign of apathy. In any case, some parent governors are likely to find themselves adrift in Board of Director-style governing bodies because as parents they have no executive or managerial function and because many feel they do not have a clear view of parental opinion in general. In any case, using the producer/consumer metaphor, what is the consumer doing in the boardroom?

A school governing body can hardly be a Board of Directors and a consumer council at one and the same time, though of course over time it may develop some of the functions of each. This highlights the essential problem of identity facing school governors, a crisis which will be resolved not by legal specifications alone but crucially through practice. The boardroom metaphor is helpful in some ways, principally because it notices governors' real power; but it is distinctly unhelpful in other ways, principally because it suggests schools are businesses. Schools certainly need the most representative and best-considered guidance from the community as a whole; and they need to be run efficiently (in a business-like way). But neither of these propositions means that schools must be run by executive directors. For one thing, governors' time is freely given and a public service as important as education ought not to be subject to the vicissitudes of voluntary labour. For another, because of geographical factors, not all schools are equally well-placed to recruit professional skills to their governing bodies. Governors seen as adding value to schools as part-time, unpaid, executives will advantage schools already advantaged in terms of their locality and its socio-economic structure.

We should be clear that governance is not a business specialism any more than it is a professional preserve.

> Our society is governed by lay people. They have professional guidance at their elbow, they rely on professionals to carry out their policies in the most effective way, but most professionals, at least in this country don't make policies. Schools are not unusual in being subject to community oversight.
>
> (Sallis, 1991: 13)

Governors as members of a jury

Sallis, a pioneer in the field, celebrates the ordinariness of governors. The thought is in favour of a body with something of the flavour of a jury. It receives expert evidence, listens to advocacy and adjudicates. School governors are not, it is to be hoped, centrally concerned with guilt or innocence but with a continuous and variegated range of educational judgements. But the virtue of plain judgement, common sense, open to professional persuasion but subject to collective decision, is what is stressed in the jury model. On such a model, governors' internal shared oversight is exercised over the functions of the school. This oversight is mainly at the level of policy to be handed over to the professionals for implementation. Conceived as non-expert policy-making bodies, school governors would indeed be appropriate forums for the political education of the populace, offering hope to those who see school governors as a locus for a rekindling of democratic participation. In such forums parents of the day would have an equal but special presence. They would be rescued from the marginality they inevitably collect in bodies conceived as executive or professional.

They would be relieved of the burden of representing 'consumers' in any strict and decisive sense; such representation is best felt in the actual market place for education, the point of recruitment for pupils, the many interactions by way of parental involvement which constitute the school's negotiations with its immediate clients.

BEYOND THE SINGLE SCHOOL PERSPECTIVE

These considerations in favour of the jury model have looked towards the relations of governing bodies with their own individual schools. The 1980 Education Act required all schools to have their own individual governing bodies for the first time. It is not surprising, therefore, that attention should have been given overwhelmingly to the local school level. Governors have been urged to support their own school, giving it its own distinctive character. But governors also have to handle external relations, with the community, with the LEA and with other agencies such as the police. In doing so, what becomes problematic once again is the governors' relation to their own school. Kogan *et al.* (1984) postulated a number of 'models' under which governors' relationships to the school and to the external environment might be understood. At the nub of such theorising is the question to what extent governors are to become part of the school, for example of its internal management, and to what extent governors are to stand apart from the school as mediators of its external relationships, for example as the bodies to which schools are in the first place accountable.

Probably the most energetic external activities governors have engaged in relate to the LEAs. Funding and staffing have traditionally (before the devolution of funding and management (LMS) consequent upon the 1988 Education Reform Act) dominated governors' external relations. Following the 1988 Act governors have had to consider opting out of the LEA altogether. Generally the thrust of these deliberations has been towards what has been for the good of the school; rarely have considerations about the welfare of the system as a whole had a hearing. Local partisanship is excusable in hard-pressed times, but could it be that the perspective afforded by governorship, the overview of one school's predicament, might encourage governors to consider alternatives to the competition among schools that is a key element in the underlying ideology of the government's educational reforms?

In other words, could we hope for governors' engagement in decisions and debates about the system as a whole? To achieve this it would be necessary for governors to escape the magnetic field of their own school for some purposes, for example by setting up federations of governing bodies. There are isolated examples of this in some metropolitan areas where competition among schools is seen to be damaging many. Also, there exist a number of agencies for inter-school relationships, such as NAGM and AGIT.

Attendance at governor training events is also a powerful opportunity for governors to compare experiences and to understand the wider situation. Just as parents find a secure place in policy-making, non-executive, non-professional, non-consumerist models, so in the wider setting parent governors' voices would be heard as part of a chorus of governors in general but complemented by specifically parental organisations such as the National Confederation of Parent–Teacher Associations (NCPTA) or, in the European context, the European Parents' Association (EPA). Sallis (1991: 6) sees it as

> inevitable that school governors will link up in clusters, neighbourhoods or whole LEA areas to share experience, promote the best practice and formulate standards. If schools *feel* like part of a local service, co-operating not competing, trying to ensure fairness to children, meeting all needs, then there *will* be a local service, whatever happens to LEAs.
>
> [original emphasis]

This optimism is part of a faith that ordinary people will reject the Social Darwinism of a government philosophy that sees improvement coming about through competition among providers (schools) in an environment of scarcity (of pupils and resources). Throughout the 1980s government sought to remove restrictions on the market for education, by opening up parental choice (actually the right to express a preference) in the 1980 Education Act, providing access to the private sector through the Assisted Places scheme, requiring schools to publish prospectuses and examination results and by publishing HMI reports. Viewed from the Tory perspective, moves towards co-operation among governing bodies might well be seen as the old restrictive practices coming back, as governors going native because they are too heavily influenced by professionals. And hence, the worry that teachers are too influential on governing bodies and ought to be restricted. Governing bodies on this scenario would have become part of the problem not part of the solution.

Much then is at stake as the new governors struggle for identity. A proper balance of interests within governing bodies has to be struck in practice. Proper relationships have to be established between governing bodies and professionals, between governing bodies and LEAs (and other agencies) and among the thirty thousand governing bodies themselves. Parent governors have an important, but not all-important, role in all these struggles. It is time therefore to turn to what we know so far of the experience of parents as governors for clues to what is to come. Two main aspects are of concern. Who are the parent governors and how are they participating?

REPRESENTATION

On representation two main sources are available. The National Foundation for Educational Research (NFER) produced an analysis of the membership of school governing bodies in England and Wales but without specific analysis of parent governors as a sub-set (Keys and Fernandes, 1990). Golby and Lane (1989) analysed the parent governor membership of primary schools in Exeter and, for comparison, the London Borough of Hounslow. The consistent thrust of these empirical researches is towards the conclusion that the educated, white, middle-class governor is in the ascendant. While women are well represented in general there are interesting variations in the gender balance between primary and secondary schools and in terms of the position of chair.

The NFER survey revealed, among other things, that:

- The governors and chairs responding to the survey were very well-qualified in terms of educational and professional qualifications. Fifty-seven per cent of chairs and forty-four per cent of the governors held either a degree or a professional institute final qualification. Very few held no formal qualifications.
- About twenty-one per cent of the chairs and eighteen per cent of the governors were employed in industry or commerce.
- About thirty-nine per cent of the governors and fourteen per cent of the chairs were employed in education/training occupations (including teaching).
- The proportion of governors (and chairs) from manual occupations was very low.

- Just over one per cent of the governors responding to the survey and about three per cent of the chairs were from ethnic minority groups.
- Approximately half of the governors but only thirty per cent of the chairs of school governing bodies were female.

(Keys and Fernandes, 1990: 33)

Golby and Lane (1989) found in Exeter primary schools that:

- Nearly one half of all parent governors come from professional or managerial backgrounds or work in education. When education ancillary workers are added in (classroom assistants, caretakers, cooks etc.), the figure increases to fifty-seven per cent.
- Of parent governors fifty-seven per cent are female and forty-three per cent male.
- The unemployed and the unskilled are poorly represented. There were only four unskilled and two unemployed governors of Exeter primary schools. No co-options were made from the ranks of the unskilled or unemployed.

They comment:

> The balance between the sexes shows that males are in the majority among the co-options and females among the parent governorships. The reasons for this demand explanation. Perhaps new governing bodies seek to redress any imbalances between the sexes when deciding their co-options. Perhaps men are simply more prominent in the local community.
>
> The dominance of professional, managerial and educational occupations among both parents and co-opted governors was perhaps to be expected. Several headteachers point out that their governors were previously well-known to the school as governors or otherwise. This points to a pre-existing network of activists in the local community from which governors are recruited. One headteacher expresses a disquiet 'Our children mainly come from an area where there is social deprivation. Although the parents wholeheartedly support the school at any event such as an Open Day, Sports Day, Parents' Evening etc and work in an informal partnership with us for the benefit of the children, they are very reluctant to take on any "official" roles. They fall over each other in their haste to get out of the

door at the end of an informal Open Evening, before the beginning of a formal meeting such as a PTA AGM'.

(Golby and Lane, 1990: 4)

This situation was seen to be mirrored in Hounslow, where, however, there was much less initial interest in the elections for parent governorships. In Exeter there were on average nearly two nominations for every vacancy while in Hounslow there were only just enough candidates to go round. Minorities are poorly represented among Hounslow governors. Many headteachers had made great efforts to recruit governors. One said she was:

> very disappointed that our parent from the ethnic minority [*sic*], did not get elected, particularly as this group represents sixty-nine per cent of our school community.

(p. 7)

From this evidence it would seem that school governorship may be an important means for some women to make a contribution but that at present there are major social imbalances in recruitment. If ordinariness is to be the major criterion for governorship then surely the net has to be cast more widely.

PARTICIPATION

The experiences of those parents who have served as governors were investigated by a group of researchers who made observations of nineteen school governing bodies (eight primary and eleven secondary) in a range of different settings, rural and urban. Something of a contrast was discovered between three-quarters of the schools where parent governors were reported to be prominent (in five schools parents had achieved the chair) and the other one-quarter of schools where parent governors were reported as unimpressive, contributing little to discussion or being dominated by other governors. Observations and interviews revealed considerable distress among the latter group.

> The evidence points to many of the silent parent governors being overawed by the weight of their responsibilities and what they perceive as the complexity and sheer volume of business which has to be dealt with in committee. They are struggling on the treadmill of modern governorship and finding its demands

daunting. For them, learning the ropes is proving problematic. A typical comment from one such governor was 'I feel our body is well run – it's all so complex and so much business. I feel peripheral and as if I am wasting time if I keep butting in to ask what it's all about'. Another parent governor had resigned from the same body prior to the study and the observer witnessed an incident in which a parent governor was 'put down' by the chair.

(Golby and Appleby, 1991: 18)

There is much else to be uncovered about parents' experiences as governors. The domination of some meetings by headteachers and chairs noticed both by Deem and Brehoney (1990) and by Golby and Appleby's researchers and the allocation of governors to sub-committees need further research. Deem and Brehony (1990: 18) say of their sample of fifteen governing bodies in two LEAs:

> Membership of finance groups is by no means representative; in five instances there are no parents at all on finance committees, while in no finance group do women governors outnumber men. Co-opted and local authority governors tend to dominate finance, marketing groups and buildings/maintenance committees, while women and parents are most likely to be on staffing, pupil and curriculum sub-committees.

Evidence such as the above suggests that the fine texture of parent governors' representation needs to be understood if they are to be supported towards full participation. Clues are perhaps to be found in the diversity of parents' experience. There may be personality factors, social factors in parents' backgrounds and factors in the context and conduct of governors' work which account for parent governors' effectiveness (as perceived by themselves and others). It will be important as a matter of principle to recognise that ineffectiveness as a parent governor may not and ought not automatically be ascribed to personal features of the governors themselves. It may be that the successful three-quarters in Golby and Appleby's research were from the chattering classes and the frustrated quarter from elsewhere. If so, a broadened recruitment of parents, which, as we have seen is much to be desired, will be to no avail if they then encounter difficulties in practice. There is, it is true, an ever greater weight and complexity of business, which many professionals find hard to cope with. But Sallis believes on the evidence of her question-and-answer column in the *Times*

Educational Supplement that some governors have to deal with obstructions. She says:

> In some schools everywhere, heads, officers, chairs of governors are disobeying the letter and spirit of the law. Perhaps they do so innocently but the effect is to impede the healthy development of the system and discourage good people.

(Sallis, 1991: 5)

WHAT IS TO BE DONE?

Given that the situation may well be serious for this experiment in small-scale local democracy, what measures may be suggested to help it on its way? A glib answer to this question is to say that training for school governorship needs to be improved. But, of course, until we are clear about the nature of governors' work and the problems they face in doing it, we cannot sensibly prepare people for it. There are numerous practical steps which would help all concerned; there are philosophical questions to be sorted out concerning the nature of governorship, its scope and limits; and there are, perhaps most important and fundamental of all, cultural changes in the ethos of schools and governing bodies which need to be identified and developed. It is not the case, however, that there is any one starting point for progress. Initiatives, changes and constraints develop simultaneously at all points in the system and we have a continuous creation of new practice out of the residue of the old.

The mainstream of broadly agreed good practice recognises this while continually pushing for improvement. The 1990 conference of the Campaign for the Advancement of State Education (CASE) considered the new responsibilities of governing bodies and the increased rights of parents to choice, information and representation deriving from legislation since 1980. The following objectives were among those agreed. They give a good flavour of mainstream agreement on good practice and they well demonstrate the interactive and organic way in which development in the work of governors must proceed.

Government should:

• consider giving governors a legal entitlement to time off with pay or loss of earnings allowance, as well as out of pocket expenses

- provide adequate funds for governor training.

LEAs and diocesan boards should:

- encourage parents' recruitment to governing bodies, providing pre-training to this end, and work for maximum participation in elections
- spread good practice among schools in communicating with parents and encouraging their help, and encourage schools to involve their governors in their daily work
- condemn bad practice in these matters
- provide a counselling and advice service both to governors and to parents
- ensure that all written information to governors and parents is encouraging and in simple language.

All schools should:

- communicate high expectations of governors, as they do of staff and pupils, particularly in the extent of their involvement in the school, their commitment to its success, their conscientious individual contributions to the governing body's work, and their effectiveness as a team
- get every governor involved in the school by establishing structures to ensure regular contact
- encourage governors to meet and communicate with parents
- share decisions in a way which involves all governors, and see governors as an internal part of the management of the school
- bring issues to governors at 'sketch plan' stage; it is not necessary to be a step ahead
- seek out and use governors' expertise
- help to ensure fairness and equality in the running of the governing body.

Governors should:

- communicate clearly with parents
- ensure that agendas and minutes are available to parents in an accessible place
- meet the parents' association regularly and attend parents' events, explaining their work to parents
- get to know the school in its day-to-day work
- in the case of parent governors, consult with parents and report back to them

- ensure parental access to the school, and encourage it in good habits of communication with parents
- establish friendly relationships with the staff of the school, 'demystifying' governors' work
- share their own work fairly and effectively among themselves
- accept that their new independence requires them to assume personal responsibility for the fair and efficient conduct of their business.

(Campaign for the Advancement of State Education, 1990)

What is striking about such a list is its undogmatic and pragmatic nature. There is here no confrontation between the educational provider and customer, no rhetoric about parent power versus the educational establishment, no overblown claims that the new arrangements will magic into existence improved standards. The political points are eschewed. So are philosophical points about parental and other rights, improved democracy, fairer representation. This is the language of ordinary people – or at least those ordinary people who work for CASE. These people are attempting to make order out of the debris of institutions and practices remaining on the ground. The LEAs exist and there is no drive here to undermine them, though some of the objectives entertained for them are patently beyond their financial powers at present. Schools' legitimate areas of action are recognised; they are not seen as on the defensive. Governors' own responsibilities, especially for good communication, are recognised but there is no theorising of the relationship between governors, schools and LEAs. The importance of relationships between governors and other bodies around the school, such as Parent-Teacher Associations (PTAs), is recognised and this is an aspect little addressed elsewhere.

In all, this is a fair intimation of informed opinion. Though fundamental questions of social policy lie just below the surface, the world of practical life presses on apace. For the future, though reforms in school governance will not usher in the revolution, they do provide the opportunity for ordinary people, coming forward as parents or otherwise, to participate in the great democracy of practice.

REFERENCES

Bacon, A.W. (1978) *Public Accountability and the Schooling System*, London: Harper & Row.

Baginsky, M., Baker, L. and Cleave, S. (1991) *Towards Effective Partnership in School Governance*, Slough: NFER.

Campaign for the Advancement of State Education (1990) 'Parents and Governors: A Blueprint for Action', *Parents and Schools* No. 59 (Winter): 8–9.

Deem, R. and Brehony, K. (1990) 'The Long and the Short of It', *Times Educational Supplement*, 13 July.

Deem, R., Brehony, K. and Hemmings, S. (1990) *The Reform of School Governing Bodies Project: A Report on the Pilot Study October 1988–March 1990*, (Occasional Paper Series No. 3) Milton Keynes: Education Reform Research Group, School of Education, Open University.

Department of Education and Science (1984) *Parental Influence at School* Cmnd 9242, London: HMSO.

Education Act 1944, London: HMSO.

Education Act 1980, London: HMSO.

Education (No. 2) Act 1986, London: HMSO.

Education Reform Act 1988, London: HMSO.

Golby, M. (ed.) (1990) *The New Governors Speak*, Tiverton: Fair Way Publications.

Golby, M. and Appleby, R. (eds) (1991) *In Good Faith: School Governors Today*, Tiverton: Fair Way Publishing.

Golby, M. and Lane, B. (1989) *The New School Governors*, Tiverton: Fair Way Publications.

Keys, W. and Fernandes, C. (1990) *A Survey of School Governing Bodies*, Slough: NFER.

Kogan, M., Johnson, D., Packwood, T. and Whitaker, T. (1984) *School Governing Bodies*, London: Heinemann.

Langford, S.G. (1985) *Education, Persons and Society*, London: Macmillan.

MacIntyre, A. (1987) 'The Idea of an Educated Public', in Haydon, G. (ed.) *Education and Values: The Richard Peters Lectures*, London: University of London.

Maclure, S. (1988) *Education Reformed: A Guide to the Education Reform Act*, London: Hodder & Stoughton.

Sallis, J. (1991) *School Governors: Your Questions Answered*, London: Hodder & Stoughton.

Shearer, A. (1991) *Who Calls the Shots? Public Services and How They Serve the People Who Use Them*, London: King's Fund Centre.

Taylor Report (1977) *A New Partnership for Our Schools*, London: HMSO.

Wilkins, J.A. (1990) 'Restructuring Education after the Reform Act – The Role of School Governors: A Headteacher Perspective', (Occasional Paper Series No. 1) Milton Keynes: Education Reform Research Group, School of Education, Open University.

Chapter 6

Parents as school board members
School managers and friends?

Pamela Munn

Parental involvement in schools has been a major strand of education policy in the UK, yet that policy has been operationalised rather
differently north and south of the border. Scotland has had radical
parental choice legislation since 1981 and the effects of that legislation have been reported by Adler in this volume and elsewhere. In
contrast, Scotland has had much weaker legislation relating to the
roles and responsibilities of school boards, Scotland's equivalent to
governing bodies. The differences extend far beyond nomenclature
and include their composition, statutory responsibilities and perhaps
their consequences for the school system.

In Chapter 5 Golby indicated the opportunities presented to
parents in England and Wales to assume co-responsibility for
school goals through the extensive powers now devolved to
governing bodies, but demonstrated that there is still a long way to
go before governors fulfil the role intended for them in terms of
both representation and participation. He also speculated about
the voice of parent governors being heard not only as part of a
chorus of governors in general but complemented by specific
parents' organisations to create a parental lobby in school matters.
Such a lobby is already developing in Scotland partly as a result of
school boards and partly because government policy has explicitly
highlighted the legitimacy of a parental voice in school affairs.
This chapter describes the intended purposes of school boards as
revealed by their composition and powers and draws on current
research evidence and recent developments to argue that boards
have developed in ways unanticipated by government. In effect
boards have largely allied themselves with the education establishment, schools, teacher unions and education authorities, in an
attempt to thwart certain education policies in Scotland. Having

created a parental lobby through the establishment of school boards and through parental choice, government has had to live with the consequences of that lobby being used in opposition to its own policies. It is important to remember in this context, that the Conservative Party holds only twelve of the seventy-two parliamentary seats in Scotland. Furthermore the rising tide of demands for devolution, if not outright independence, for Scotland has made education a highly sensitive policy issue. Together with the church and law, education is seen as a pillar of Scotland's nationhood and culture. Some opposition to Conservative policy, for example, has been mounted on the slogan that the 'Englishing' of Scottish education is underway. Whatever the rights and wrongs of such opposition, it needs to be borne in mind in considering the evident distrust of government policy evinced by some parents' groups.

SCHOOL BOARDS' POWERS AND COMPOSITION

The 1988 School Boards (Scotland) Act came into force on 1 April 1989. The Act provides for every local authority school in Scotland (except nursery schools) to have a school board. Latest figures show that two thousand three hundred and forty-eight schools throughout Scotland now have boards, a total number which means that ninety-six per cent of secondaries, eighty per cent of primaries and forty-seven per cent of special schools now have boards (Scottish Office, 1991). Boards for individual schools have been in existence only a short time in Scotland, unlike school governing bodies south of the border where the 1980 Education Act ensured that each school would have its own governing body. Perhaps their shorter life in Scotland goes some way to explaining the rather more limited powers assigned to them than those conferred on governing bodies in England and Wales by the 1988 Education Reform Act. Governing bodies in England and Wales have powers to hire and fire school staff, for example, and extensive powers over the general financial management of schools, with local education authorities statutorily bound to devolve at least eighty-five per cent of their budgets to their schools by 1993. In contrast school boards' functions are:

- to promote contact between the school, parents and the community and to encourage the formation of a parent–teacher or parents' association

- to approve the headteacher's plans for use of the capitation allowance (typically the budget for books, stationery, equipment etc.)
- to participate in the selection of senior staff
- to control the use of school premises outside school hours
- to set occasional holidays during term time
- to receive advice and reports from the headteacher and, in particular, an annual report which includes a report on the aggregate level of pupil attainment
- to have any matter raised by the board considered by the headteacher and education authority
- to receive information from the education authority about education in the area, including statements about past and intended expenditure on schools.

A glance at the functions specified for school boards reveals the very limited nature of their formal powers. If the role of managers is seen as taking strategic decisions about the future direction of an enterprise and creating a context in which employees can most effectively get on with the job, then it is clear that school boards have a very limited managerial function. In key areas of school life such as the curriculum, assessment policy and practice, admissions policy, staffing, homework and discipline, boards have no decision-making power. They have the power to ask questions, monitor performance and make representations to the headteacher and staff, the local authority, and central government about these areas, thus opening up possibilities for exerting influence, but this is rather different from managing schools. Indeed, the areas under the direct control of boards are sparse, involving administrative rather than educational matters. Although few would deny the need to have efficient administration of school letting and of the setting of occasional holidays, these are hardly the life blood of schools.

Boards' powers in the area of school finance are also limited, concentrating on giving approval to headteachers' plans for buying books and equipment and in managing their own internal board budget. Local financial management of schools has not yet arrived in Scotland, where local authorities still control and manage school budgets. Experimental schemes to devolve financial management have been tried in two regions, the massive Strathclyde Region and the more sparsely populated Dumfries and

Galloway. In each of these rather different schemes, budgetary power has been devolved directly to the headteacher, not to school boards.

In part boards' limited powers are a reflection of their much shorter history in Scotland than in England and Wales. They have been in existence for only two years and replaced the largely discredited school councils which were concerned with a group of schools, typically a secondary and its associated primaries (see Macbeth *et al.*, 1980 for a full discussion of the role of school councils). Boards' powers also reflect the overwhelming response to the consultation exercise about their composition and function, carried out by the then Minister of State for Education in Scotland. The consultation exercise proposed 'floor' and 'ceiling' powers, for boards, the latter being more akin to the powers of governing bodies. There was widespread public and professional reaction against the 'ceiling' powers, and the school board legislation essentially incorporated the 'floor' powers while including a provision for boards to ask local authorities to delegate more responsibilities to them. It is worth noting that no board has, as yet, availed itself of this opportunity.

Although Conservative government policy has given Scottish school boards rather fewer powers than those exercised by English governing bodies, it has emphasised the centrality of parental influence in school affairs through the composition of board membership. There are various categories of membership – teacher, co-opted and parental – but the statutory composition of boards is such that parents are in the majority. Not only are they the largest single group; they outnumber all other categories of membership combined. Thus if a matter came to a vote at a board, all parent members, if present and if voting together, could prevail over any other combination of membership. The precise number of board members in each category depends on the number of pupils on roll (see Table 6.1). It should be noted that the head-teacher is principal professional adviser to the board, not a member, and that the Director of Education or his nominee has the right to attend and speak at meetings, as does the Regional or Islands councillor in whose ward the school is situated. Board members, then, have few real powers but potentially they could be influential. How have parent members used their influence?

Table 6.1 Composition of boards

	Number of pupils			
	1–500	*501–1000*	*1001–1500*	*1500+*
Parent members	4	5	6	7
Staff members	1	2	2	3
Co-opted members	2	2	3	3

Note: Single teacher schools will have 3 parents and 2 co-opted members but no staff members since the single teacher is the headteacher.

BOARDS' SUPPORT FOR SCHOOLS

Government pronouncements about the aims and purposes of boards stress three main functions: the greater involvement of parents in school affairs, closer community involvement with schools and freeing education authorities progressively from the business of routine school administration. These aims were encompassed within a broader aim of realigning the balance between producer and consumer rights in public services to enhance the latter. School boards are an attempt to increase consumer influence and rights on schooling (parents acting as guardians of their children's interests) against these of the producers, schools and local authorities. Or are they? Boards' powers to ask the education authority for information on almost any educational matter, and especially their power to ask for an annual report from the headteacher, can be seen as making these education producers more accountable and as shifting the balance towards an explicit recognition of the legitimacy of the consumers' interests. The government's suggestion that boards should ask headteachers for reports about the school curriculum and about the level of pupil attainment imply, however, that boards are to perform a monitoring role for the government. That is, boards are intended to act as the government's agents in ensuring that schools are kept up to the mark. In other words, the ultimate producer of schooling, government, tells the consumers, boards, what their interests should be. The government has assumed that its interest in improving school quality and in raising standards of pupil attainment and crucially *in its policy for achieving these ends* will be shared by consumers. The attempt by government to harness parental support for its policies has been largely unsuccessful in Scotland. Instead of consumer voices challenging producers, they have sided with them to challenge government education policy.

Evidence from the pilot school boards set up by Dumfries and Galloway a year in advance of the first statutory boards (Munn and Holroyd, 1989) and from observation of a number of meetings of the statutory boards (Arney *et al.*, 1992) reveals that board members tend to be strongly supportive of their schools. This support took the form of explicit statements of support, such as 'this school is a great wee school', but was also conveyed in a marked reluctance to challenge the headteacher. Indeed the few challenges observed during the course of the two research projects have been easy for the headteacher to crush. For example, one parent on a primary school board raised the issue of the amount of homework being expected of pupils. She reported that several parents had expressed concern that too much homework was being set and that it was unrealistic to expect young pupils to devote a significant amount of time to it. The headteacher, supported by the teacher representative on the board, politely but firmly told the parent that homework was an area outside the board's competence, and this was accepted by the chair. While making decisions about homework policy is clearly outside the statutory duty of boards, making representation about it certainly is not. The board's reluctance to challenge the headteacher may have been due to a hazy grasp of board powers or to an unwillingness to rock the boat in a school that was highly regarded. Headteachers for their part have been assiduous in providing reports on various aspects of school life, often proposing that these appear as items on the agenda. Such reports have included pupil achievements, curriculum provision, and subject choices for senior pupils in secondary schools. The tendency of boards is to note these reports with very little discussion of their content and very little cross-examination of the headteacher. A detailed analysis of board business over twenty-six meetings revealed that boards spent almost thirty per cent of their time on procedural matters. Educational matters also had a high profile as Table 6.2 shows.

It is noteworthy that the headteacher was the principal source of information on education matters. The analysis of the outcomes of the sixty-nine items of educational business reinforces the view that members are very reluctant to challenge the heateacher. Of

Table 6.2 The business of boards observed

Type of business	Percentage of time to nearest whole number	Principal source(s) of information
Procedural	28	Chair Region
Educational	19	Head
Home–School	18	Members Head
School–Community	9	Head Region Members
Buildings	8	Region Head
Finance	7	Region
Training	5	Training Co-ordinator Colleges Region
Staffing	3	Head
Other	3	

these sixty-nine items, thirty-one were noted without discussion. These were usually headteacher reports which were received with nods of approval. In two boards where individual members were clearly determined to question or comment on headteachers' reports, a general discussion involving other board members did not usually ensue. These individuals were very much on their own. Of course, it is impossible to generalise from the small number of boards (fifteen) which have been observed to all school boards in Scotland. However, the evidence is consistent with larger-scale surveys of parental views (Scottish Office Education Department, 1990) which reveal a general trust in the professional expertise of teachers and a belief that schools are doing a good job. So boards have not acted as a thorn in the flesh of schools; rather they have been harnessed to support schools and to put pressure on education authorities for more resources.

Perhaps the latter was a role which government did indeed expect boards to play, challenging education authority policy and practice. In contrast to the reluctance to challenge their headteachers, boards have had few inhibitions about cross-examining education authority officials about financial allocations to schools and the rationale for these allocations. Boards are sympathetic to headteachers' concerns about the lack of money for books and equipment and are generally shocked at the low level of per capita allocation, especially in primary schools. The lack of spending on school maintenance, repairs and decoration is highly visible to board members whose meetings are typically held in the school and who tour school premises from time to time as part of their duties. The need for parents to subsidise educational visits has also been debated.

Less visible to boards is the quality of the day-to-day teaching and learning in schools. Nevertheless, the general trust in teachers' professional expertise and the traditional view of education in Scotland as a collective welfare right for all have been reflected in boards' suspicions of government policy enabling individual schools to opt out of local authority control. Boards' concerns that opting out might lead to a two-tier state education service to some extent lie behind the fact that no school in Scotland has yet opted out.

It is ironic that government, having explicitly set out to create a parental voice in school affairs through parental choice and school boards, has had to live with the consequences of this voice being raised in opposition to its own policies and in support of schools. The issue which has aroused most parental opposition has been the introduction of national testing for primary pupils aged eight and twelve. (There is no compulsory testing of fourteen- or sixteen-year-olds in Scotland.) School boards have not been in the forefront of organising parental opposition to national testing although some individual members have played a prominent role. In the small number of primary school boards observed as part of research on school board training, the issue became an increasingly dominant concern. Worries were voiced that testing would serve no useful purpose and be disruptive of children's learning and, especially, that it was the beginning of a return to selective schooling. In the event, there was a large-scale parental boycott of national testing during the pilot run in April 1991. Parents withdrew their children from schools on test days or wrote to headteachers instructing them not to administer the tests to their children (*Scotsman*, 1991; Strathclyde Regional Council, 1991). The Parents' Coalition which led the boycott renewed its campaign in 1992 and some leading members of the coalition are also members of school boards. In the 1991 boycott, parents had the explicit support of Scotland's largest teaching union, the Educational Institute of Scotland, and the support, sometimes tacit, sometimes overt, of the education authorities (almost all of whom are Labour controlled). Far from parental influence being exerted to make schools and education authorities more responsive to consumer concerns, it has been exerted to influence government policy with parents siding with local producers against the national producer. Parents' groups have not been slow to hammer home the legitimacy of their consumer interest.

INDIVIDUAL BOARDS, LOCAL AND NATIONAL FEDERATIONS

Parental opposition to national testing was widespread, and forcibly demonstrated the power of collective action. Will boards consider the possibilities of collective action, through the formation of local and/or national federations? If so, what would be the probable focus of such collective action? Such limited research evidence as is available in Scotland suggests that the concerns of a board tend to be with its own school. Boards are interested, for example, in the condition of *their* school buildings, *their* school's facilities and *their* school's capitation allowance. When boards ask education authorities for information about, say, their repair and maintenance programme, it is typically in order to lobby for their own school to be moved up the list or to argue for more money for their school. This is understandable and rational. Parents are most concerned about the school their own children attend rather than the generality of schooling. However, if school boards are to provide the stimulus to active citizenship and local democracy which both Golby and Raab in this book envisage, then parental involvement has to extend beyond concern for a specific school, to a general concern with schooling locally and nationally. This is so for three main reasons.

Firstly, school board members can only understand the specific situation in their own school by understanding the broader local and national education policy context. If boards want things to change and improve at school level, they need to know who has the power to make things happen, so that they can lobby effectively.

Secondly, a failure to see schooling as a common interest is likely to reduce ability to influence events. Boards in competition with each other will, to borrow from Golby, be losers and losers, as division will open up possibilities for education producers to play boards off against each other.

Thirdly, active citizenship and local democracy imply a concern with local society and communities which extends beyond a specific school. Even in the narrowest definitions of community, the communities of a secondary and its associated primaries need to take account of each other's problems and concerns – out of self-interest if nothing else.

In Scotland a number of local federations of school boards are now in existence, and a national association or federation is in the process of being born. It is still too early to say anything about their role, far less their effectiveness, but indications are that they are going to concentrate on big issues, such as curriculum, assessment and resources. This does not mean that boards will cease to be interested in and concerned about their own school. Far from it. Rather, that as they have gained in experience, they are able to see where real power lies. However, to maximise their effectiveness boards need to be able to claim that they in some sense represent the parental voice. Is this the case?

BOARD MEMBERS AND PARENTS IN GENERAL

In this section I want to consider two aspects of representation: how representative parent board members are in terms of the generality of parents and how board members keep in touch with parents about their concerns.

Information about parent members is sparse. A survey of members of seven pilot school boards (Munn and Brown, 1989) found that over a third were neither past nor current Parent–Teacher Association (PTA) members; nor had they other links with schools or with the education service in general. Boards had tapped previously uninvolved parents and this was welcomed. Men and women were equally represented although there were more men on secondary school boards. This picture proved to be unrepresentative.

Findings from a national survey of a representative sample of two hundred board members revealed the following:

- Both parent and co-opted members came predominantly from A, B, C social classes; semi-skilled and unskilled workers were vastly underrepresented.

- Men and women were equally represented, though women predominated in primary and special schools. Boards showed a tendency to elect male chairs.
- Members' professional involvement in education was more frequent than would be expected among the general community. Some thirty-seven per cent of parent members had worked in education at some time (MVA, 1992).

The picture tends to be similar to that in England and Wales. The educated, white, middle-class board member is in the ascendant in Scotland too. How have these board members kept in touch with parents?

Board members have made numerous efforts to communicate with parents, including:

- newsletters
- social functions, such as barn dances, wine and cheese parties
- being available at parents' evenings/school open days
- distributing questionnaires to parents asking them to list their priorities for or concerns about the school
- meetings on school premises to discuss particular issues.

These efforts have been largely unsuccessful and boards are now more jaundiced and cynical about parental interest. One parent in the study by Munn and Holroyd (1989: 11) reported that board members had been approached by only two parents during a parents' evening where parents discussed their children's progress with teachers. He remarked ironically:

> I think we were approached because we were just happening to be sitting near the tea urn ... available for people waiting to see the teachers.

Unsurprisingly, it has been easy to mobilise parental action when a real problem or threat to the school is evident, closure being the obvious example. It can be inferred that most parents will become active when there is something to be active about. Getting them involved in routine business is difficult. And, interestingly enough, more recent research on school board training revealed that materials on *Links with Parents* had been used by twenty-six per cent of respondents who had used any training units (Arney et al., 1992).

An area still to be researched is the relationship between school boards and parents' or parent–teacher associations. Members of these associations are to be found on boards, and act as channels of communication between the two. In other instances, particularly in small schools, the setting up of a board has led to the demise of the parents' association as there are insufficient parents to support both. Unfortunately, no data are available on the number of parents' associations set up or disbanded as a consequence of boards.

IMPLICATIONS OF SCHOOL BOARDS FOR EDUCATION AUTHORITIES

What are the likely consequences of school boards for education authorities? Paradoxically, one short-term consequence has been an increased workload. The existence of school boards has led to the establishment of school board units in each authority whose remit is to act as a channel of communication between the boards and the authority, provide training opportunities for board members and generally act as troubleshooters. The units vary in size and are staffed at varying levels of seniority. Most either have direct access to senior officials through the unit head or are themselves headed by an Assistant Director of Education.

A second short-term consequence already mentioned has been to make authorities more directly accountable to parents through school boards. New financial management systems, identifying schools as individual cost centres, have enabled boards and head-teachers to compare schools' budgets. Boards have been un-pleasantly surprised at the low levels of per capita allocations to schools and have not been slow to ask for detailed explanations of budgetary allocations. Comparisons with neighbouring school budgets have had similar effects. Education authorities, therefore, are likely to be confronted with demands from school boards for additional resources for their schools. Inevitably, some boards will be more skilled and successful in pressing these demands than others and so school boards may increase inequality in educational provision, especially if local and national federations of boards do not develop.

A longer-term consequence for education authorities is likely to be less concentration on the minutiae of financial management and a far greater devolution of budgets to schools. The experiments already under way in Strathclyde and Dumfries and Gallo-way give headteachers greater control over some aspects of the school budget such as staffing costs, repairs and maintenance, and supplies and services. It is interesting that these experimental schemes devolve decision-making to the headteacher, not to the school board. In the context of greater devolution of financial management the role of the education authority is to provide central services such as that provided by educational psychologists, teachers of children with special educational needs, advisers and the like. Either such services might be 'bought' by schools according to the headteacher's perception of need, or an authority might decide to retain a proportion of the education budget to provide a specified level of such services in all schools. The increasing financial autonomy of schools in England and Wales and the then Education Minister's enthusiastic account of the local management of schools in New Zealand, following a visit there in April 1991 (*Glasgow Herald*, 1991), strongly suggest that the Conservative Party intends that Scottish schools are to have greater control of their budgets. Whether this control will be exercised by the head-teacher or school board remains to be seen. Whatever the outcome, it seems that board members can hardly be described as school managers. They have shared goals with their schools and sometimes with the education authority and teachers' unions, bringing their own distinctive pressure to bear as a way of achieving these goals.

What also remains to be seen is the configuration of alliances among the various education partners: central government, education authorities, teachers' unions, school boards, and parents' groups. The signs so far in Scotland are that parents' groups and parents' associations have joined education authorities and teachers' unions to protest against central government policy on national testing. On local issues, schools and school boards have united to put pressure on the education authority. We shall no doubt see a changing constellation of partners depending on the issue. What is certain is that the parental lobby, strengthened by legislation on school choice and school boards, is here to stay. Whether the partnerships now in evidence will continue in the event of greater parental management of schools in Scotland is a matter of debate. The continued parental trust in the professional expertise of teachers suggests that government, whatever its political complexion, may have to contend with a parental lobby which will cause them greater problems than teachers or education authorities. School boards are schools' friends.

REFERENCES

Arney, N., Munn, P. and Holroyd, C. (1992) *The Provision and Take-up of School Board Training,* Edinburgh: Scottish Council for Research in Education.

Education Act 1980, London: HMSO.

Education Reform Act 1988, London: HMSO.

Glasgow Herald (1991) 'Visit to New Zealand Hardens Forsyth View on More Independence for Schools', 26 April. See also *Scotsman* (1991), 'Forsyth's Secret Schools Shake-up', 17 April.

Macbeth, A.M., MacKenzie, M.L. and Breckenridge, I. (1980) *Scottish School Councils: Policy Making, Participation or Irrelevance?* Edinburgh: HMSO.

Munn, P. and Brown, S. (1989) *Pilot School Boards: First Impressions,* Edinburgh: Scottish Council for Research in Education.

Munn, P. and Holroyd, C. (1989) *Pilot School Boards: Experiences and Achievements,* Edinburgh: Scottish Council for Research in Education.

MVA (1992) *Study of the Work of School Boards: First Interim Report,* Edinburgh: MVA.

School Boards (Scotland) Act 1988, Edinburgh: HMSO.

Scotsman (1991) 'Almost Half Strathclyde Parents Shun Test', 6 March.

Scottish Office (1991) 'School Board Elections', *Statistical Bulletin* Edn/B8/1991/3 (May).

Scottish Office Education Department (1990) *Talking about Schools: Surveys of Parents' Views on Schools and Education in Scotland,* Edinburgh: HMSO.

Strathclyde Regional Council (1991) Information Release, Education Department, 8 March.

Chapter 7

Parents as partners
Genuine progress or empty rhetoric?

John Bastiani

There has never been a more opportune, challenging or exciting time for those who would like to see more effective relationships between families and schools. For a number of developments have occurred, whose combined impact is likely to have a far-reaching effect upon current thinking and practice in this area. Relationships between families and their children's schools, and the longer-term *consequences* of these relationships, have become a key issue for everyone with an interest in the educational service – politicians, professionals and parents alike – albeit in widely differing and often contradictory ways.

Firstly, there is considerable cumulative evidence of an uneven but definite spread of changing parental attitudes to and expectations of their children's schools. This is allied to, and reinforced by an increase in the numbers and range of parent groups and organisations.

Secondly, it is now possible to catalogue with conviction, and support with clear evidence, some of the advantages and benefits that improving relationships between families and schools can bring, particularly for pupils themselves. What for a long time has seemed to be a mixture of faith and optimism, laced with odd bursts of support from research and development work, now has a more consistent and sharper empirical edge.

Finally, there is a compelling and inescapable need for professionals to review both their thinking and their practice in the light of new statutory obligations and far-reaching political directives which permeate family–school relations, as elsewhere. However, this is far from straightforward. At times, the new legislation seems to be supportive of forward thinking and the development of effective practice. Often, however, the new requirements appear to threaten and undermine much that has been achieved in recent years and to be based upon competing claims, ideas and values that not only appear to have tenuous links with the real world, but also seem to be profoundly contradictory and flawed.

This chapter sets out to briefly explore some of these issues and contradictions and the challenge they present for the development of thinking and practice, against the background of a broad view of the current scene and of recent achievements. Above all, it seeks to examine and unscramble some of the rather loose and widely used rhetoric of partnership and its implications, not only for teachers, parents and pupils, but for all those who wish to see these partners working together more effectively.

The surge of current political interest in relations between parents and their children's schools and the consequent working through of legal and contractual requirements and professional obligations might give the impression that home-school matters are a newly discovered area. Nothing, however, could be further from the truth.

There is currently, for example, something of a 'rediscovery' of the crucial importance of the relationships between family expectations, social background and educational achievement, although this rediscovery has been used to pursue a market-forces approach to schooling. The new emphasis on home–school relations needs to be seen not only against earlier major researches in this area, but also in the context of the continuing efforts of many schools and families, trying to work together more effectively, often against considerable odds. The following section serves as a brief reminder of the importance of the family's influence upon pupils' educational attainments and their participation in further and higher education.

FAMILY AND SOCIAL BACKGROUND, SCHOOL EFFECTIVENESS AND PUPIL ACHIEVEMENT

Firstly, there is plenty of evidence (e.g. Mortimore and Blackstone, 1982) of the mutually reinforcing nature of social and educational disadvantage. There is now also clear evidence that the gap between the most disadvantaged families and neighbourhoods in the UK and the advantaged has widened considerably during the last decade.

At the same time, there has been an underlying shift of emphasis in social policy, at all levels, from the needs of families during the formative years of childhood to the needs of the economy and the achievements of school leavers. Here, the continuing influence and long-term effects of family attitudes towards 'staying-on' rates and towards participation in further education and training have been emphasised by a series of very unfavourable comparisons with school leavers in other advanced economies.

Similarly, current attempts to disentangle the combined effects of social background and other pupil intake factors are part of a strenuous professional response to government requirements to publish tests scores and examination results, without any commentary or adequate interpretation (Nuttall and Goldstein, 1989).

Although recent and earlier evidence meshes with both the everyday experience of ordinary teachers and sheer commonsense in showing that family influences are paramount, there is now convincing evidence that 'schools matter'. Research, based on large-scale, cross-phase studies in the UK, Australia and the USA, shows that schools in which pupils 'do well' (as defined by a series of measures of both achievement and positive behaviour) are *all* characterised by 'good' home–school relations (Brighouse and Tomlinson, 1991).

These successful schools go well beyond the basic legal requirements to develop effective, two-way communication, are accessible in a variety of ways and at all reasonable times, work hard to find ways in which parents can encourage and support their children and provide them with practical help and, above all, build a sense of shared identity and common purpose – the beginnings, at least, of a genuine partnership.

To the possibilities of an educational partnership offered by the 'effective schools' research, we can add the massive and combined efforts of many initiatives, from a number of LEA-funded projects (mainly in England), to school-based initiatives, often carefully planned and monitored, where the driving force has been the systematic involvement of parents in their children's reading development and, more recently, in schemes to develop children's mathematical abilities (Hannon *et al.*, 1985).

These initiatives, which probably owe much to the fact that reading and mathematics continue to be major concerns for teachers, parents and pupils alike, have done much to influence professional attitudes and to convince families and schools of the value of mutual co-operation. For it shows, without any doubt, that when teachers, parents and pupils work together, in a spirit of practical partnership, then not only do pupils gain in obvious ways, but there are also benefits of achievement and relationship that are both lasting and transferable to other aspects of children's learn- ing and development.

THE *IDEA* OF PARTNERSHIP

For me, a striking feature of the term of 'partnership' is the huge discrepancy between its common usage and any careful consideration of its possible meanings. 'Partnership' is a term widely used throughout the education service, to cover a range of situations and circumstances. Its use, or overuse, is more often than not uncritical, implying that it is highly desirable, unproblematic and easily attainable.

A few moments' thought, by contrast, reveals a set of interpretations that are hard to grasp, intellectually challenging and, above all, extremely difficult to realise in practice. Indeed, it might be more appropriate to talk about *working towards partnership*, as being a worthwhile direction, rather than something which is commonplace.

In view of its common usage, there have been surprisingly few attempts to pin down partnership in educational terms. Here are three versions of the idea, which I have found helpful in drawing attention to its differing aspects. The best known of these is from Pugh (1989: 5), whose work is based on the pre-school years which, together with the field of special needs, are the areas where genuine partnership is most likely to be found.

Her definition is particularly useful in identifying the requisite knowledge, attitudes and skills, and refers to 'a working relationship, characterised by:

- a shared sense of purpose
- mutual respect, and
- a willingness to negotiate.

It implies a sharing of information, responsibility, skills, decision making and accountability.'

The second definition, drawn from Mary Drummond's unpublished speech to the 1991 North of England Education

Conference, stresses the processes of communication and the need for links between words and actions. For her, effective partnership is about:

• doing things, not talking about doing things
• the need to talk to each other, but even more to be able to disagree
• listening to each other
• taking full responsibility for what each does, both singly and together.

The third definition, from Wolfendale (1989), embodies her particular interest in the special needs field and her focus is on the need to translate clear policies into effective action. For her, partnership entails being:

• involved in decision-making and its implementation
• perceived as having equal strengths and equivalent expertise
• able to share responsibility, so that parents and professionals are accountable to each other.

These contributions, which contain both overlapping and distinctive emphases, suggest to me a view of partnership, in which there is:

• sharing of power, responsibility and ownership – though not necessarily equally
• a degree of mutuality, which begins with the process of listening to each other and incorporates responsive dialogue and 'give and take' on both sides
• shared aims and goals, based on common ground, but which also acknowledge important differences
• a commitment to joint action, in which parents, pupils and professionals work together to get things done.

PARTNERSHIP IN ACTION: SOME CURRENT INITIATIVES

The idea of a developing partnership between families and schools has provided both the rationale and the substance of a number of significant funded projects and initiatives throughout the UK. The Parent–School Partnership Initiative in Liverpool, the Strathclyde Partnership Project, based in Glasgow, the Coventry and Humberside Community Education Projects and, more recently, the Royal Society of Arts Partnership Project, based in London, have accumulated much valuable experience, survived a number of threats to their existence and continue to highlight the value of family–school co-operation.

Other, equally successful, projects have been less fortunate. The Woodside Project in Telford, the Haringey Home–School Project in London and the Oxford Partnership Programme have, together with a number of other, less well-known projects, fallen victim to financial retrenchment.

All such initiatives, however, have been affected in one form or another. They have been obliged to seek alternative homes and funding, to 'go underground' or, commonest of all, to spread their energies and resources across ever-wider territory or to scale down their operations to the point where their effectiveness is greatly reduced.

Like everything else these days, too, home–school initiatives are also obliged to justify themselves to close scrutiny and control, to the exigencies of performance indicators, to a continuing 'audit' of their costs, benefits and measurable outcomes. This sometimes sits uncomfortably alongside their original spirit and approach, but their continuing survival itself often depends upon demonstrating success in terms of clearly measurable improvements in pupil performance.

To their credit, the best initiatives appear to have reconciled these conflicting agendas and to have made a virtue of necessity, offering valuable experience in generating new ideas and making them work, in contributing to the review and evaluation of existing thinking and practice, and in pinpointing areas of growth and development. They encourage the movement towards two-way communication and practical partnership, and lead the way by example.

It has been a feature, though not always a condition, of funded home–school work in the UK, that it has been characterised by a special concern for those parents and families who, for a variety of reasons, need most support and encouragement in dealing with their children's schools. Finally, such initiatives have kept alive, against constant threat, a wider view of education which is concerned not only with children's learning in classrooms and schools, but with the broader education and development of families and their communities.

SOME OBSTACLES TO PARTNERSHIP

In spite of the considerable achievements and benefits of home–school co-operation, briefly outlined in previous sections, any realistic appraisal of the current scene has, inevitably, to recognise that future progress in this area is likely to have to come from individual schools themselves. This will be largely the result of their own commitment and effort and will itself be under threat from counter-influences and pressures. In this section, some of these obstacles will be briefly examined.

Whilst the government clearly espouses the benefits of the partnership, its policies and actions seem to be flawed by a number of powerful contradictions. In its legislation throughout the 1980s the government appears to be strengthening the role of parents, especially in the management of their children's schools. For some parents, however, especially those in difficult circumstances, the combined effects of charge capping, formula funding through the local management of schools, and the redefinition of Home Office-funded Section 11 schemes in multi-ethnic settings have meant the reduction and sometimes the axing of home–school liaison schemes and work.

Similarly, the government, through its commitment to market values and mechanisms, endorses the notions of parental choice and improved standards through competition. In reality, however, open enrolment and the introduction of generously funded forms of covert selection, through opting out of local authority control and the introduction of City Technology Colleges, have institutionalised competition between schools for parents and between parents themselves for scarce school places.

This view of competition within a consumerist model of the delivery and consumption of educational services is entirely antithetical to the notion of educational partnership in which parents and teachers share the responsibilities as co-educators, celebrate achievements together and collaborate to tackle problems and difficulties. This is based upon the assumption that the education, welfare and development of young people are too complex and too difficult for either to tackle alone.

Finally, the government has, throughout the last decade, imposed a view of schooling that is limited, instrumental and dominated by a concern with regulation and control. Parents may ostensibly have rights to express a preference for their choice of a school, but they have virtually no say over what their children learn, how they are taught or how assessed since the legislation means, in effect, that schools compete in providing the same kinds of curriculum and assessment. Research on parents' views of schools (e.g. Elliott *et al.*, 1981) shows that whilst parents value a school's academic record they also endorse the need for schools to share responsibility for a child's well-being, healthy development and social adjustment.

CHANGING PROFESSIONAL ATTITUDES

In order to review some of the complexities of the current scene, it is useful to approach it from different angles and perspectives. In this section, I seek to summarise basic professional attitudes that have been characteristic of the education service throughout the UK. Such underlying attitudes have been embedded in teachers' thinking, are deeply ingrained in their behaviour and are remarkably persistent. Whilst such attitudes *are* slowly changing, the changes are extremely ragged, uneven and, to an extent, unpredictable. Such attitude changes have been uncovered by National Foundation for Educational Research (NFER) national surveys in England and Wales (Jowett and Baginsky, 1991) and by a number of home-school research and development projects. Above all, however, professional attitudes are *implicit* in the substantial and diverse home–school literature and in the everyday experience of families with school-aged children in their dealings with schools.

Table 7.1 summarises a range of attitude changes which suggests a *general* shift of stance and perspective.

THE CHANGING EXPECTATIONS AND EXPERIENCE OF PARENTS

As a number of important studies during the last decade (Atkin and Bastiani, 1988; Elliott *et al.*, 1981; MacBeath *et al.*, 1989; National Consumer Council, 1986) have shown, parents' educational beliefs and expectations, their actual dealings with their children's schools and their wider involvement in parental concerns, are not only enormously diverse, but also susceptible to change in the light of experience.

Table 7.1 Changing professional attitudes: a summary

From	*To*
Parents are a problem (and often a nuisance) • They are either 'not interested' or they are 'too interested', i.e. interfering. • They take up time and energy that should be spent working with children. Teachers should be allowed to get on with the real job of teaching. • Teachers/parents should get on with their own respective jobs.	• Parents have (increasingly) clearly defined rights – and obligations – in respect of their children's schooling. • Schools cannot survive without the active involvement and support of parents. • Teachers and parents both have key roles in a shared enterprise. • Schools have a legal, contractual and professional obligation to work with (all) parents.
Home–school relations are: • Mainly for those who work with young children – or those with special needs. • Peripheral to the main business of the school. • Essentially concerned with teachers and parents. • Mainly concerned with relationships between individual families and their children's schools.	• Important for all schools. The long-term consequences of family–school relationships have an important bearing on young people's achievements and attitudes to further education and training. This is a key European issue. • Right at the heart of the educational process in general, and pupil achievement in particular. • Necessarily involve pupils. • Need to be supported by collective parental representation.

Improving home–school work is:
 • Simply a matter of developing 'good practice'.
 • More about being seen to act than about thinking through the nature of home–school relationships.
 • Working with parents is something that you learn 'on-the-job', from experience. Training is unnecessary.
 • Not a priority. Schools are best placed to bring about their own continuing development.
	• 'There's more to it than meets the eye!'
	 • Need for thoughtful 'whole-school approach', based on an analysis of current practice.
	 • Improving your work with parents is a key task for initial training, INSET and professional development.
	 • Yes – but they need the encouragement and support of the educational service as a whole, and of parents. There are issues of:
	    – policy and legislation
	    – resources
	    – training
	    – evaluation and development.

Amongst parents as a whole for instance, there has been a slow, but definite, shift of attitudes away from deference and a widespread sense of helplessness, towards a recognition that parents do have formal rights regarding the provision of information, some rather basic opportunities for access, and some representation in formal decision-making, however obscure. In spite of such subtle but significant changes, widely reported but difficult to pin down, there is equally obviously a long way still to go.

Clearly, too, many if not most schools have become dependent (as several major independent studies in England and Wales have recently shown) upon the goodwill, the practical support and, particularly, the financial contributions of parents. Apart from its general effect upon family–school relationships, often subtle and difficult to establish, this growing financial dependence marks further sources of tension in the redistribution of power and responsibility within the education system. It also exacerbates already huge inequalities of provision between schools and neighbourhoods.

As far as parent representation and parent organisations are concerned, there has been a rapid growth, both nationally and locally, in the number, size and range of organisations representing different aspects of parental interest and experience. Amongst the better-known national groups in England and Wales, the National Confederation of Parent–Teacher Associations (NCPTA), for example, has more than eight thousand school branches in its federated districts; the Advisory Centre for Education (ACE) reports big increases in both the number and kinds of parents seeking information and advice about their children's schooling; the Campaign for the Advancement of State Education (CASE) continues to organise effectively across a range of issues of concern to parents of school pupils. And so on.

The position with regard to the emergence of new pressure, interest and support groups is more difficult to track, especially if one takes a broader interest in the education, welfare and development of children and young people, rather than a narrow concern solely with school-related matters. At present, parents have little or no power base, either as individuals or in organised groups, at school, local or national levels. Whilst there are clear and promising signs that this is changing, these efforts remain largely uncoordinated, under-developed and inadequately resourced.

In spite of the rhetoric, parents of children in the UK currently lack a clear agenda, a mandate for action and the political clout that is needed to bring about far-reaching change. The time is now certainly ripe for initiatives that will not only make more effective use of existing activity and achievement, but also enable parent groups, of widely differing kinds, to get together to influence the setting of national educational agendas and to begin to work in real partnership with professional bodies and with the educational service as a whole.

Perhaps too, there are lessons to be learned from an active participation on the wider European scene, where the efforts of national parent organisations appear to be more co-ordinated, within and between member states and are more positively supported bv their national governments. Recently, for example, a French initiative via Centre Européen de Parents de l'École Publique (CEPEP) has attempted to identify a common philosophy and an agreed approach to issues of parent representation and teacher training, whose aim is to work towards a partnership between the two (Tomlinson, 1991).

THE RHETORIC OF PARTNERSHIP ITSELF

Unscrambling the relationship between rhetoric and reality, between strongly held beliefs, politically motivated claims and the realities of everyday, lived experience, between what we say and what we do, is complicated. The following very different examples, drawn from the arenas of both policy and practice, illustrate something of the complexities of the rhetoric of partnership with parents, both as a set of ideas and as a springboard for action.

> We often talk about the partnership in education. Of course parents have a right to expect schools to provide good education, and that is why we are undertaking radical reforms of the education system. But perhaps we lay insufficient stress on the responsibilities of parents in that partnership. Teaching is a difficult enough task made even more difficult when parents don't take their responsibilities seriously enough.
>
> (Baker, 1987)

> It is hoped that a genuine partnership between parents and their child's teacher will grow. To foster this, the school has a Parent–Teacher Association, which aims to hold social evenings, to raise money and to nourish the growth of links with the community.
>
> (1990 primary school brochure for parents)

A fruitful partnership between home and school would seek to:
- encourage a shared commitment to the success of the individual child;
- create an ethos of understanding and openness in home–school relationships;
- help parents to develop a positive role in complementing and supporting the work of the school in educating their children.

Their aims are likely to be realised by:
- providing opportunities for the free flow of information in both directions;
- encouraging dialogue and the interchange of ideas and opinions;
- seeking parental co-operation in planning the range of experiences which home and school should together provide for pupils;
- involving parents in the process of determining the way forward for their own child's education; informing parents and developing with them an understanding of assessment and recognition of achievement of their children;
- recognising the developing and changing role of the pupil in the process of negotiation.

> (National Association of Head Teachers 1990:1)

But this is to devalue and distort the notion of partnership. Partnership depends upon and recognises the similarities and differences of each partner. There is overlap between the roles and expertise of teachers and parents, but there are distinct areas that are the prerogative of each. Thus, partnership does not seek to merge these into a mish-mash of confused roles but to celebrate both the overlaps and the distinct areas. It seeks also to get a better balance between the two, and to see how they can be classified and articulated to each partner. In short it is a means of establishing relationships in which both partners are respected and trusted, can communicate easily and clearly, and are working together towards the same end – a more effective and appropriate education for children.

> (Community Education Development Centre, 1988)

HOME–SCHOOL PARTNERSHIP: A MOVING TARGET?

'Partnership' is one of the most dominant and widely used images of our times, not only in education but also elsewhere. Any attempt, however, to examine it as a set of ideas or practices, quickly reveals its complex and elusive nature. This section attempts to explore some of its characteristics as a necessary starting point for any attempt to monitor or evaluate existing practice or to encourage the further development of thinking and action in this area. This is done in the belief, firstly, that it is necessary to have a clearer understanding of some of the opportunities and problems involved to be able to work towards more effective practice and, secondly, that we need a clearer idea of the consequences if we are to bring intentions and achievements closer together.

Everyone's in favour of home–school partnership – whatever it is! But because it's a buzzword, there also tends to be a conspiracy to avoid looking at it too critically in case it falls apart or disagreements break out! Partnership is easy to talk about, much more difficult to achieve in practice. Genuine progress is often uneven and inconsistent, difficult to pin down or evaluate and sometimes seems to be swapping an old set of problems for a new set.

In the real world, there are important differences of attitude and expectation not only between parents and teachers but also amongst them. So partnership inevitably means different things to different people. It can range from simple forms of co-operation between home and school to joint planning, teaching and evaluation of the curriculum.

Perhaps it is more helpful to see partnership as a process, a stage in a process or something to work towards rather than something that is a fixed state or readily achievable. In this context, there have been a number of interesting attempts to see home–school relations as a wide range of varied possibilities characterised by ground rules that reveal different patterns of authority and relationship and different ways of working. In some cases, these were concerned with the development of a signed agreement which set out parents' and teachers' understandings of their respective roles in relation to children's school work; in others the focus was upon introducing parents into classrooms to help with reading or information technology. Finally, there is the argument (familiar in fields like community development but not so much in education) that 'partnership' is not, in any case, an appropriate or adequate model. Focusing upon the everyday lived experience of poor and powerless families in inner cities, of ethnic minority families, of single parents and of others, supporters of 'advocacy', for example, argue that more radical and drastic measures and even structural changes are needed before partnership could ever begin to be considered as a possibility – if at all (Phillips, 1989).

PARTNERSHIP: SOME WAYS FORWARD

This account has presented some of the difficulties likely to be encountered in bringing families and schools together into a genuine and effective partnership.

However, there is also a growing feeling amongst those who are involved with and committed to home–school work that the government's emphasis on parental involvement in schools provides an opportunity for some national initiatives in this area. Here are three suggested starting points:

- Identify a genuinely parental agenda. This would need to incorporate consultation with a wide range of groups and agencies. Above all, however, it would need to tap into a broad cross-section of the views and experience of parents as a whole.
- We need to review the present home–school scene, in the light of the spirit and agreed principles of educational partnership. This would need to be wide-ranging and concern itself with the different needs of both the educational service and the life of families.
- Above all, we need to 'model' partnership in action in different ways and at different levels and see what happens. This might include the following: setting up, monitoring and evaluating activities involving collaboration amongst teachers, parents and pupils; disseminating positive examples and good practice; sharing the experience of partnership in action warts and all; sponsoring training in home–school relations for both teachers and parents; and identifying criteria of good practice in home–school relations.

Home–school partnership cannot be left to quietly evolve, unaided, in its own good time! Neither should it be left to individual schools, teachers and parents to foster on their own, without help. It is a major task that calls for imagination and commitment, initiative and direction; it also needs management, understanding and support. There is, here, an important role for policy and legislation, a need for appropriate resources and a key task for both initial training and further professional development. We also need to harness some of our growing skill in reviewing present thinking and practice and learn some of the lessons which our individual and collective experience teaches us, in order to move forward.

REFERENCES

Atkin, J. and Bastiani, J. (1988) *Listening to Parents: An Approach to the Improvement of Home–School Relations*, London: Croom-Helm.

Baker, K. (1987) The Churchill Lecture, Cambridge, December, quoted in National Association of Head Teachers (1990) *The Home–School Contract of Partnership* (A discussion paper), Haywards Heath: National Association of Head Teachers.

Bastiani, J. (1987) *Perspectives on Home–School Relations: Parents and Teachers* vol. 1. Windsor: NFER-Nelson.

Bastiani, J. (1989) *Working with Parents: a Whole-School Approach*, Windsor: NFER-Nelson.

Brighouse, T. and Tomlinson, J. (1991) *Successful Schools* (Education and Training Paper No. 4), London: Institute for Public Policy Research.

Community Education Development Centre (1988) *Parents and the Education Reform Act*, Coventry: Family Education Unit, Community Education Development Centre.

Community Education Development Centre (1991) *Partnerships With Parents in the Primary School: Activities for Staff and School Development*, Coventry: Family Education Unit, Community Education Development Centre.

Elliott, J., Bridges, D., Ebbutt, D., Gibson, R. and Nias, J. (1981) *School Accountability*, London: Grant McIntyre.

Hannon, P., Nutbrown, C. and Weinberger, J. (1985) *Involving Parents in the Teaching of Reading: Some Key Sources*, Sheffield: Department of Education, University of Sheffield.

Jowett, S. and Baginsky, M. (1991) *Building Bridges: Parental Involvement in Schools*, Windsor: NFER-Nelson.

MacBeath, J., Mearns, D. and Smith, M. (1989) *Talking about Schools: Surveys of Parents' Views on School Education in Scotland*, Edinburgh: HMSO.

Macbeth, A. (1988) 'Research about Parents in Education', in Brown, S. and Wake, R. (eds) *Education in Transition: What Role for Research?* Edinburgh: Scottish Council for Research in Education.

Macbeth, A. (1989) *Involving Parents*, London: Heinemann.

Mittler, P. and Mittler, H. (1982) *Partnership with Parents: Developing Horizons in Special Education*, Stratford: National Council for Special Education.

Mortimore, J. and Blackstone, T. (1982) *Disadvantage and Education*, London: Heinemann.

National Association of Head Teachers (1988 and 1990) *The Home–School Contract of Partnership* (A discussion paper), Haywards Heath: National Association of Head Teachers.

National Consumer Council (1986) *The Missing Links between Home and School: A Consumer View*, London: National Consumer Council.

National Home–School Development Group (In preparation) *Making Partnership Work: Some Materials for Teachers*, Nottingham: School of Education, University of Nottingham.

Nuttall, D. and Goldstein, H. (1989) 'Differential School Effectiveness', *International Journal of Educational Research* 13.

Phillips, R. (1989) 'The Newham Parents' Centre: A Study of Parent Involvement as Community Action', in Wolfendale, S. (ed.) *Parental Involvement: Developing Networks between School, Home and Community*, London: Cassell.

Pugh, G. (1989) 'Parents and Professionals in Pre-School Services: Is Partnership Possible?' in Wolfdendale, S. (ed.) *Parental Involvement: Developing Networks between School, Home and Community*, London: Cassell.

Tomlinson, S. (1991) *Teachers and Parents* (Education and Training Paper No. 7), London: Institute for Public Policy Research.

Topping, K. and Wolfendale, S. (eds) (1985) *Parental Involvement in Children's Reading*, London: Croom-Helm.

Wolfendale, S. (1989) 'Parental Involvement and Power Sharing in Special Needs', in Wolfendale, S. (ed.) *Parental Involvement: Developing Networks between School, Home and Community*, London: Cassell.

Chapter 8

Home–school relations
A perspective from special education

Seamus Hegarty

The ideology of partnership, which has become endemic in considerations of home–school relations, is subjected to scrutiny and found wanting. This chapter opts for a functional description of home–school relations. It examines home–school relations in special education in five areas: communication; curriculum; assessment; personal support; and liaison with other agencies. Such an approach is held to be more useful because it allows for the possibility of partnership but is not confined to partnership-type activities.

THE PROCRUSTEAN BED OF PARTNERSHIP

Mary Smith and John Jones are parents of pupils at Elm Vale Secondary School. Both pupils have special educational needs. Mary, a consultant paediatrician, sits on the school governing body and is an extremely articulate member. John is a long-term unemployed labourer who left school at fifteen and can barely read.

To say that relations between home and school are likely to be very different in the two households is to state the blindingly obvious. If one goes beyond that however to suggest that they *should* be different, problems arise. Such pragmatism challenges the prevailing orthodoxy of partnership between home and school. In particular, it sits uncomfortably with the Warnock espousal of parents as 'equal partners in the educational process'.

There are in fact substantial difficulties with the notion of parents as partners in their children's schooling, and in particular with the way in which the ideology of partnership is bandied about. Firstly, if parents relate to schools in many different ways, it becomes difficult to see in what sense they are all partners. Which aspects of the relationship constitute partnership? Is it governing or fundraising or helping in the classroom? Presumably, not everything counts: if partnership is used to mean anything from acting as school governor to receiving adult literacy tuition, the concept becomes so all-encompassing as to be vacuous. If there is a core set of activities which define partnership, are those parents who participate in them partners, and the others not?

Secondly, when schools are seen as just one of many service systems in modern society, the notion of partnership becomes less central. Indeed, it begins to look suspiciously like a hangover from older, rural models of society where self-sufficiency was the norm but which – for good or ill – no longer match how people live. The individual in modern society interacts with numerous service providers: banks, utilities, refuse collectors, healthcare systems, social services and so on.

These interactions are not usually seen in terms of partnership. The normal basis is one of contract: a service is specified and, on payment of agreed fee, delivered. (This applies no less to public sector services such as education and health where payment is indirect, through taxation or social insurance.) The mechanic who services a car or the solicitor who conveyances a house is not a partner. They are experts, who are paid – and thereby bound by contract – to carry out specific tasks. This is associated with the fact of specialisation and its corollary, dependency. The mechanic could in principle conduct a conveyancing just as the solicitor could learn to service a car. In general, however, most people content themselves with acquiring a limited repertoire of skills and accept their consequent dependence on others' skills.

The implications for teaching are clear. Educating a child is not the same as servicing a car or conveyancing a house – actually, it is far more challenging but teaching does not stand outside the framework of service provision in contemporary society. Those aspects of education conducted in school rely on expertise, particularly where pupils with special educational needs are concerned, and are the responsibility of paid professionals. Much education goes on outside school, of course, and is the proper domain of parents. Schooling is quite distinct from education and is likely to be deskilled and undervalued if there is a too easy partnership between parents and teachers.

Thirdly, the respective roles of parents and teachers are so different as to greatly limit the relevance of partnership to an analysis of the relationship between them. The teacher's involvement is professional, lasting for a limited period of time, based on expertise, concerned with many children and exercised within the relatively artificial world of the school. By contrast, the parent's involvement is personal, lifelong, based on common-sense and emotional commitment, focused exclusively on that child and deployed in the home and the community.

The two sets of roles are complementary and elements of genuine partnership may be found in them. However, there is far more to the relationship between home and school, and attempting to squeeze its full richness into a procrustean bed of partnership inevitably leads to distortion and loss of perspective. There can and should be an equality of regard between parents and teachers, but that does not constitute partnership nor does it necessitate subscribing to a pseudo-egalitarian rhetoric of partnership.

There is an alternative approach and that is to go for a functional description of home–school contact. This entails asking: What activities does it consist? What purposes do they serve? How do the different aspects relate to each other and to the overall goals of schooling? How do they relate to parents' wishes and needs? Such an approach allows for the possibility of partnership, where that is an appropriate form of relationship, but is not dependent on it nor confined to it.

In this chapter five forms of home–school contact are discussed: communication; curriculum development and implementation; assessment; personal support; and liaison with professional agencies.

COMMUNICATION

Good lines of communication between home and school are paramount and should suffuse all the other activities. Communication and the exchange of information need, however, to be considered on their own as well and form the starting point for any consideration of home–school relations. Parents and teachers inhabit very different worlds and view the child from different perspectives. Unless there is a deliberate, sustained effort to bridge the two worlds, the likelihood is that the child's education will suffer.

The flow of information between home and school should be two-way. Over and above basic information on any relevant medical matters, the school has to become informed on the child's learning difficulties and the wide range of factors which have a bearing on them. Some of this information will emerge at school through the child's responses to learning tasks, but teachers can also learn a great deal from parents about the child's pattern of difficulties and what the parents can do – and maybe are already doing – to help.

Teachers must not lose sight of the fact that learning difficulties are usually construed to mean difficulties in learning at *school.* While school learning is undoubtedly important, it is not the only learning that people do. Attention to this fact in the light of information on how children learn outside school may give teachers a broader understanding of how individual children do actually learn and help them to provide more productive learning experiences in school.

Teachers benefit also from knowing about the home background and any relevant factors in it that affect a pupil's response to schooling. When pupils live in difficult home situations it is imperative that teachers are aware of this so as not to exacerbate problems inadvertently. Aside from such circumstances, it is helpful to be aware of the family's attitude to the child, what expectations it has, how it regards the child's difficulties and copes with them and, above all, the personal resources it can bring to supporting the work of the school.

The flow of information from school to home is no less important. Parents of children with special educational needs should have received a good deal of information before they come into contact with the school. They should have been given an understanding of the nature of their child's difficulties and the educational implications of any impairments they may have. They should have been made aware of local facilities and, in particular, the educational provision available for pupils with special needs in the area. They should know which schools have particular expertise or make provision which may be appropriate for their child. (See Consumer Congress, 1991 for an action guide.) Alongside all this, they should have access to a named individual who can provide information and advice on the available options.

Schools may well have to supply some of this information themselves either directly to individual parents or by feeding it into an information network, but they have to provide much more information when a child is starting school – or when parents are trying to choose a school. The 1980 Education Act lays a duty on schools to publish sufficient information to enable parents to make informed decisions about them. Parents' rights to receive information were increased by the 1986 Education Act and are set to be further enhanced by the Parent's Charter.

At the moment, however, the information given on special needs provision is often sketchy and has to be supplemented if it is to be of use to parents. This information should of course cover the curriculum and arrangements for assessment, but it should also tell parents about the ethos of the school, how it treats its pupils and what it expects of them. It should lay the groundwork for parental involvement by outlining to parents the range of possibilities and explaining to them the part they can play.

It is one thing to accept that communication between home and school is important and even to agree what topics it should cover. It is quite another matter to achieve it in practice. The best practice is likely to encompass a range of means of communication: written materials, face-to-face dialogue, group meetings, school open days and home visits.

The role of documents and written information is sometimes underestimated. Certainly, on their own they can be a limited form of communication and are necessarily one-way, but they do have certain advantages which other forms of communication lack. Written information is permanent and can be referred to repeatedly in order to deepen understanding or clarify ambiguities. Because of its permanence, it also tends to be more public and thereby subject to scrutiny; this in turn puts a premium on both accuracy and relevance. Examples of information that parents should receive in written form include assessment outcomes, curriculum statements, school procedures and reference data. These documents should be developed with parents' information needs in mind and, if possible, in collaboration with them to ensure maximum intelligibility. This may seem such an obvious requirement as to be hardly worth stating, but a random sampling of school curriculum statements, for instance, leaves one wondering how well they are targeted at a parent audience.

Whatever written information is available needs to be supplemented with oral presentations and, where appropriate, with opportunities for dialogue where parents can relate the information being conveyed to their own situation. The formal language of curriculum statements may mean very little to some parents, whereas an informal question-and-answer session can give them a good idea of what is going on in their child's classroom.

Not only are such occasions important in enhancing parents' understanding, but they also enable parents to draw attention to unwarranted assumptions and point out gaps and irrelevances in the information provided. School open days are another valuable source of information about school: parents, like everybody else, understand better what they experience at first hand, and the opportunity to observe classrooms in action can convey more about the curriculum than hours of being talked at about it.

Home visits are a good means of exchanging certain types of information which it may be difficult or even inappropriate to commit to paper. Such visits can be an extension of informal dialogue taking place in school – not least because parents are on their own ground and may feel able to raise questions or voice concerns that they could not air in school – but they also provide teachers with valuable insights into the real situations of families. They can see how the family copes with their child's special needs and gain an understanding of its philosophy of life and its expectations for that child. They can assess the personal resources the family can bring to bear in supporting the child's schooling. Without the insights gained in this way it is sometimes difficult, if not impossible, for teachers to involve parents in their child's schooling or to monitor the effectiveness of the overall school programme.

Good communication between home and school has many benefits. Apart from laying the foundation for more sustained collaboration, it promotes the sense of a shared enterprise. It is particularly helpful for parents to know that there is mutual understanding and exchange of information and that the information they themselves have to offer is taken seriously. It also helps in anticipating problems and resolving them when they do arise.

CURRICULUM

The central task of schools is to facilitate pupils' learning. When pupils have difficulty in learning, this task becomes if anything more important. The curriculum is therefore a principal arena for home–school contact and one where effective links between home and school can do much to enhance children's education.

There are many programmes designed to involve parents in delivering the curriculum (for recent overviews, see Bastiani, 1989; Jowett and Baginsky, 1991). These are mostly school-based but, where pupils with special educational needs are concerned, home-based activity is no less important. Some of these children function at a low level academically and need a great deal of practice and reinforcement in order to master even basic concepts and skills. Work during the school day on language and behaviour patterns may be wasted or even prove counterproductive unless backed up appropriately outside school. Most important of all, many of these children are critically dependent on highly structured learning environments; they have a reduced capacity to learn from random stimuli, and benefit greatly from having learning experiences structured in a consistent way across the whole day.

There are many home-based ways of involving parents in the curriculum. These can be for the purpose of ensuring that the work of the school is carried on or reinforced at home or of facilitating parents in making their own input to the curriculum. Such initiatives range from highly structured activities such as Portage to *ad hoc* and informal contact. Portage is a home-teaching programme that involves parents and professionals in carefully planned programmes (White and Cameron, 1988). It covers a wide range of early development and lends itself to working systematically through agreed aspects of development. These cover language, cognition, social development, self-help and motor activities. Extensive materials including behavioural checklists, teaching suggestions and activity charts are available. From its origins in Wisconsin in the late 1960s, it has spread around the globe and has been a channel of services for tens of thousands of children with disabilities.

Other formal programmes are often focused on language, with parents reinforcing and supplementing school work in the natural language situations arising at home. If pupils are using a signing system to communicate at school, they benefit from the opportunity to practise using it at home. There are of course numerous initiatives on parental involvement in pupils' reading (Smith, 1987; Topping and Wolfendale, 1985). Most of these do not refer explicitly to children with special needs but they do provide a useful body of practice which can be drawn upon.

A school's input to home can also be relatively unstructured. Some schools make use of home–school books for carrying out specific activities at home and building on the work done in school. They can be the basis of regular daily or weekly homework or they can be a means of reinforcing particular pieces of work on an occasional basis. They can also be used to ask parents about particular activities in the home or obtain feedback on specific programmes. Many schools appreciate the importance of enlisting the support of parents and ensuring that they back up the work of school – providing good models for speech, stimulating the child appropriately, reinforcing independence programmes and not colluding in immature behaviour.

Most of these activities are teacher-directed and parents are very much the junior partners – if indeed they are partners at all. Many parents are perfectly happy with this: their child's education is problematic, and they look to teachers for expertise and specific guidance on what they can do to help. As experience with Portage has shown however (Bishop *et al.*, 1986; Cameron, 1988; Mindell, 1988), parents can take on active roles – refining and modifying curriculum objectives, devising new ways of meeting them, changing repetitive practice of basic skills into fun-filled family activities. Teachers should be aware of this potential and take whatever steps they can to realise it.

Parental involvement in the curriculum can also take the form of input by parents to the work of school. Parents can contribute to curriculum planning by developing, in discussion with teachers, a more detailed understanding of their children's strengths and weaknesses, what teaching approaches are likely to be effective with them, and how they are actually responding to various approaches. This contribution can be made in a more formal way if parents are given a say in curriculum design or sit on curriculum planning groups, though this is not yet common practice.

Parents can also play a significant role in the delivery of the curriculum in school. At a basic level, they can provide an extra pair of hands in the classroom, thereby giving teachers more teaching time and allowing them to give more individual attention to children. Parents can also help in implementing teaching and therapy programmes if given appropriate instruction and specific tasks to carry out.

Some caveats need to be entered. Firstly, not every parent is in a position to become involved in this way. Some may not have the time or the inclination, and some indeed may not be suited to work in the classroom. Secondly, care must be taken to maintain the distinction between home and school in the child's perception. Pupils with special educational needs need parents as well as teachers; if a particular parent is making a major input to the classroom and taking steps to carry on the work of the school at home, there is a danger that schooling will loom too large in the child's experience. Thirdly, the relationship between parents (and other voluntary workers) and paid staff needs to be considered. Issues to be resolved include the threat to waged jobs, the school's deployment of the funds available to it, and the relative competence and commitment of voluntary workers.

ASSESSMENT

Assessment can be one of the most fraught aspects of home–school relations but it is also one where close collaboration yields great benefits. The sources of the tensions are clear enough. Assessment as an activity brings the lay/professional divide into sharp focus, and the use of formal testing procedures and technical language tends to exclude parents. Moreover, the outcomes of assessment can have very evident practical implications for how children are taught, or even where they are taught; if parents are unhappy about the outcomes, but are powerless to play any part in how these outcomes are arrived at, it is inevitable that tensions and frustrations will result.

Parents have the potential to make a major contribution to assessment. They see and interact with their children in many different situations, and have a great deal of tacit knowledge about them. They may lack expertise and be unaware of how to interpret what they observe; they may have no experience of children with similar patterns of behaviour and be so bound up in their own child's problems that they have difficulty in standing back and taking a balanced perspective. However, this should not debar them from making a major input to the assessment process. They have a unique experience of their child which, properly harnessed, can modify and enrich the more focused insights of the professionals.

The challenge to teachers and the other professionals concerned is to find ways of involving parents in assessment and enabling them to make a real contribution. The first requirement is an attitudinal one: teachers must believe that parents have a valuable role to play and that it is worth listening to them. Parents may need help in articulating their views if they are unused to the kind of reflection entailed or lack the appropriate language.

The formality of case conferences and the statutory assessment procedures can be very off-putting for some parents, to a point even where their rights to information about what is going on are rendered ineffective. Teachers can help here by ensuring that parents receive the requisite information, in good time and in an intelligible form. They can act as mediators or interpreters between parents and other professionals: they are more likely to see parents regularly and be able to initiate easy dialogue with them. They also have opportunities to explain technical language by referring to specific examples of children's learning or behaviour.

Parents can play a major role also in the school's monitoring of their child's progress. Teachers will of course be concerned with pupils' responses to teaching programmes and should be collecting systematic feedback on them. On their own, however, they have no information on how the effects of school programmes generalise to pupils' lives outside school. Parents can provide this information so far as the home is concerned and probably for some other non-school situations as well. This is critical to evaluating the school's work with the child and establishing how well the skills and insights acquired at school are transferred into other contexts.

Aside from the fact that they spend so much time in the company of their children and can observe naturally how they apply school learning in new situations, parents can be primed to look out for particular matters. This can help them to focus their observations and relate them to current work in school. In the case of very specific behaviours, teachers may provide a simple observation schedule – in the style of Portage – to assist parents in observing and recording behaviour.

Regardless of what they observe or how they do it, parents need to give feedback to teachers if the latter are to benefit from their observations. They can do so by means of home–school books, occasional chats with the teacher or formal review meetings. Some schools make a point of having review meetings on a regular basis where everybody involved with the child has the opportunity to make an input. When parents are enabled to participate in such meetings, not only can they hear teachers' and others' reports at first hand – and if necessary question them – but they can also place their own observations and suggestions before the group.

PERSONAL SUPPORT

Bringing up a child with special needs can be difficult, and some parents need support as individuals in their own right. This is different from the support given through information and advice that enables parents to play an effective role in their child's education. It is rather to acknowledge the range of demands made upon them that can go far beyond what most parents may expect. This does not entail treating them – any more than their children – as totally special cases. Nor does it imply that bringing up a child with disabilities is necessarily a negative experience for families; as Powell and Ogle (1985) and others have noted, many families testify to the positive impact of their experience of disability. There are times however when some parents benefit, both in their role as parents and as collaborators in their child's education, from a degree of extra support and understanding. This can come from the professionals involved with their children, who for the most part are teachers, and from other parents.

Teachers can play an important role in assisting parents to view their children realistically and accept their limitations. They are possibly in a unique position to do this since parents relate more easily to them than to other professionals and also because teachers are more likely to discuss the child in terms that the parents can understand. Because of their experience teachers are well placed to help parents take a long-term perspective. Parents, of course, have a long-term awareness of their own child that no one else can have, but the very intensity of this does sometimes mean that they are overcome by present difficulties. This is where the teacher who is concerned and informed but not emotionally involved can assist with a necessary balance and detachment. In some situations the teacher's role is simply to be a sympathetic listener. Teachers must be careful here since they are not usually trained to provide counselling or social work support and in any case seldom have the time to do it properly. There will be occasions, however, when simple humanity demands that teachers provide a shoulder to lean on because nobody else with the necessary detachment is available.

Support of a different kind is provided by contact with other parents of children with special needs. Their common experiences enable them to understand and support each other in mutually helpful ways. This can take the form of straightforward social contact, simply giving parents the sense of belonging to a group, or it can be an opportunity for sharing experiences and providing mutual reassurance and encouragement. Some schools make special efforts to facilitate contact between parents through coffee mornings, open days and the like or through support for formal self-help groups such as the Parent to Parent scheme (Hornby, 1988). Integration can help in this respect since, while the total number of parents of children with special needs may be less than in a special school, they are likely to have readier access to the school. It also tends to lead to the informal contact that is so valued by many parents.

LIASION WITH PROFESSIONAL AGENCIES

Many pupils with special needs are involved with health and social services as well as education, and a given family may have dealings with a large number of agencies. This presents problems for both parents and school. For parents it can mean relating to a large number of professionals, an experience many find confusing if not intimidating. As far as the school is concerned, it becomes only one of many agencies dealing with the pupil and not necessarily the most authoritative one. Teachers have a significant go-between role here and can provide a valuable link between parents and professionals. They can help parents to find their way around the system, explain their rights to them and interpret official information and reports. They can also assist in practical ways such as facilitating appointments, helping with transport and securing allowances.

Many of these functions fall outside the teacher role as normally conceived. Teachers may feel that they have neither the time nor the expertise to carry them out properly. The question then arises whether they should be carrying them out or not. Certainly, teachers could fulfil this role if they were timetabled for it and given the necessary training. A critical consideration must be what happens when parents are given no support in their dealings with professional agencies. On past experience, the likely result is that many will continue to play a marginal role in their child's schooling and will not gain full benefit from the services available to them.

The Warnock Report (1978) did in fact envisage such a role. It proposed that all parents of children with special needs should be able to look to a 'named person' who would 'provide them with a single point of contact with the local education service and expert counsel in following their child's progress through school' (9.27). It recommended that for most children the named person should be the headteacher of their current school or another staff member who was versed in special needs education. It was hoped that this recommendation would be incorporated into the 1981 Education Act but, despite considerable lobbying by parent groups, it was in the end excluded. Whether or not this work is recognised and resourced, it still needs to be done. If nobody else is concerned to do it, it falls – as with much else – to the lot of individual teachers to do it as best they can.

CONCLUSION

Rejecting partnership as the central dynamic of home–school relations may seem excessively pragmatic, if not cavalier, but there should be no hesitation in doing it. Some sacred cows are more use dead than alive. Slaughtering this particular cow does not detract from or limit the possibilities inherent in home–school collaboration. If anything, it opens them up by throwing off a mental straitjacket and, by making way for a functional description, facilitates a more focused scrutiny of what actually happens and can be made to happen.

Take communication, for instance. It is all very well to regard the Smith and Jones households as partners with the school, but it is considerably more useful to ask what their respective communication requirements are and how they are best met. There will almost certainly be differences between the two households. Effective communication is important in both cases and the basic principles governing it may be the same, but the ways in which it is realised will be very different. Mrs Smith, for instance, is likely to have a better understanding of any underlying medical factors than teachers and could well explain these to staff. Mr Jones on the other hand may have the greatest difficulty in understanding even the most basic facts about his child's learning difficulties even when they have been explained to him repeatedly. Similar observations could be made about parental involvement in the curriculum, in assessment and so on.

Partnership may be an agreeable concept, redolent with egalitarian overtones, but the warm glow of right thinking should not be confused with dispassionate action carefully designed to achieve significant targets. It is for these reasons that it has been set aside here. What the Smiths and the Joneses and all the other parents in their situation need is a meaningful involvement in their child's schooling so that the very different contributions of home and school work together in the child's interests.

REFERENCES

Bastiani, J. (1989) *Working with Parents: A Whole-School Approach*, Windsor: NFER-Nelson.

Bishop, M., Copley, M. and Porter, J. (eds) (1986) *Portage: More than a Teaching Programme?* Windsor: NFER-Nelson.

Consumer Congress (1991) *Choosing a Mainstream or Special School: An Action Guide for Parents*, London: Consumer Congress.

Cameron, J. (1988) 'Portage: The Parents' Voice', in White, M. and Cameron, R.J. (eds) *Portage: Progress, Problems and Possibilities*, Windsor: NFER-Nelson.

Education Act 1980, London: HMSO.

Education Act 1986, London: HMSO.

Hornby, G. (1988) 'Launching Parent to Parent Schemes', *British Journal of Special Education* 15(2): 77–8.

Jowett, S. and Baginsky, M. (1991) *Building Bridges: Parental Involvement in Schools*, Windsor: NFER-Nelson.

Mindell, N. (1988) 'Changes in Parental Attitude Following Involvement in Portage', in White, M. and Cameron, R.J. (eds) *Portage: Progress, Problems and Possibilities*, Windsor: NFER-Nelson.

Powell, T.H. and Ogle, P.A. (1985), *Brothers and Sisters: A Special Part of Exceptional Families*, Baltimore, Md.: Paul A. Brookes.

Smith, P. (ed.) (1987) *Parents and Teachers Together*, London: Macmillan Education.

Topping, K. and Wolfendale, S. (eds) (1985) *Parental Involvement in Children's Reading*, London: Croom-Helm.

Warnock Report (1978) *Special Educational Needs*, Department of Education and Science, London: HMSO.

White, M. and Cameron, R.J. (eds) (1988) *Portage: Progress, Problems and Possibilities*, Windsor: NFER-Nelson.

Chapter 9

Ethnic minorities
Involved partners or problem parents?

Sally Tomlinson

Although government policies during the 1980s have cast parents primarily in the roles of consumers, managers and agents of competition, rather than as partners in the education process, it is now becoming more widely accepted that positive parental involvement and partnership with schools is one of the prerequisites of effective schooling and that co-operation between home and school can raise educational achievement. Accordingly, there is now considerable interest in encouraging parents to participate more directly in their children's schooling, to give parents more access to information about education, and to develop more structured home–school links.

Given the relationships that ethnic minority parents have had with schools over the past thirty years, it is likely that the involvement of these parents as genuine partners in education will be more difficult to achieve than that of white parents. Racial and cultural differences have added an extra dimension to problems of home–school relationships. Minority home–school encounters have perforce taken place in a society marked by racial antagonisms and intercultural tensions rather than by harmony – and teachers, who have not been well equipped during their training to deal on a professional level with ethnic minority parents, have often clung to negative, stereotyping and patronising views. The research literature into the 1990s suggests that educational professionals still regard ethnic minority parents as posing problems for schools, rather than as assets in the educational process.

This chapter examines misunderstandings which still characterise relationships between ethnic minority parents and schools, and the stereotypes many teachers still hold of ethnic minority households. The chapter notes assimilationist and nationalistic pressures which do not help teachers to regard ethnic minority parents as equals and to respect their views and needs. It describes recent research in which Bangladeshi parents were interviewed about their views on education and contacts with schools, to illustrate some of the problems encountered by ethnic minority parents in becoming informed about and involved in their children's education. Ethnic minority parental representation on governing bodies is particularly noted. The chapter concludes with some recommendations for bringing ethnic minority homes and schools closer together.

A GULF OF MISUNDERSTANDING

Those parents who migrated into Britain from the Caribbean, the Indian sub-continent, East and West Africa and Hong Kong had been educated in colonies in which education promised power and money, and they had high expectations of the education systems their children were entering. Research from the 1960s consistently demonstrated that schools and their children's education were a matter of great concern to ethnic minority parents. Most migrant parents did not enhance their own levels of qualifications or skills by migration, but were eager for their children to benefit from education and obtain good qualifications and employment. While they did not necessarily aspire for their children to be professionals, they did expect them to be given the means to be occupationally secure (Rex and Tomlinson, 1979).

There has, however, been a mismatch of expectations between what ethnic minority parents expected of education, and what teachers felt they could offer. During the 1970s, ethnic minority parents became increasingly anxious that schools should equip their children with skills and credentials to compete with white pupils, and the issue of achievement became a dominant concern, particularly for Caribbean parents, whose children were consistently regarded as likely to be low achievers. Ethic minority parents also expressed their desires that their backgrounds and cultures be respected and ethnic minority cultures taken seriously in schools. Some Muslim parents for example found themselves increasingly in conflict with a co-educational secularised system but found schools unresponsive to their wishes (Parker-Jenkins, 1991). This mismatch of expectations did not necessarily lie in teacher obtuseness, but rather in the structures and functions of the education system. Ethnic minority children usually entered urban schools which were not equipped to prepare pupils for higher level academic work or, until the advent of the Technical and Vocational Education Initiative (TVEI), technical work. Teacher expectations of pupils whose backgrounds, cultures and languages they did not understand have been consistently low, and this has persisted as a generation of British-born young ethnic minority pupils have entered schools (Smith and Tomlinson, 1989). Parents who initially lacked knowledge and information about the school system placed an inordinate faith in teachers, and many were disappointed with both the processes and the outcomes of schooling.

Teachers have always had difficulty in communicating with ethnic minority parents. Townsend and Brittan (1972) reported that, out of two hundred and thirty multi-racial schools they studied, over half found problems in establishing personal contact with parents. Rex and Tomlinson (1979: 204), after studying schools in Handsworth, Birmingham, reported that:

> One thing that does emerge from this research is that the immigrant parents' expectations of schools and the definitions of their children as problems by both educational policy-makers and teachers will produce a situation of misunderstanding at best, and direct conflict at worst.

By the early 1980s ethnic minority home and school relations were in a critical period. The Rampton committee of inquiry into the education of ethnic minority children wrote in its interim report that a 'gulf of mistrust and misunderstanding' appeared to be growing between schools and parents, and parents had lost faith in schools to make improvements (Rampton Report, 1981). Some parents' groups were suggesting short-term segregated schooling, and a black supplementary school movement was flourishing (Tomlinson, 1984, 1985). In London black parents had become more vocal in their dissatisfaction – one group in Haringey writing to local headteachers to accuse them of 'failing miserably' to educate a substantial number of black children (Venning, 1983).

During the 1980s, ethnic minority parents, in common with other parents, benefited to some extent from improved home–school contacts. They also benefited from legal requirements in the 1980, 1986 and 1988 Education Acts which gave parents more rights to information about schools, access to curriculum documents, governors and HMI reports, and equal representation on governing bodies. Some urban schools in areas of high ethnic-minority settlement have been in the forefront of pioneering more imaginative home–school contacts, and the development of local education authority and school policies on multicultural, anti-racist education during the 1980s included much consultation with ethnic minority parents.

Kate's Hill primary school in the West Midlands, for example, is one of twenty schools taking part in a home–school project supported by the Royal Society for Arts (RSA) and the National Association of Head Teachers (NAHT). This multi-racial school has a well-developed community philosophy and a network of outreach developments, including an Asian parents' group, a parent–toddler group, a toy library, a family day and at home visiting. The school has developed contracts with parents, committing the school to value each child as an individual, explaining curriculum and reading programmes, and holding regular meetings to discuss children's progress (*Home–School Contract of Partnership Newsletter* 1991). Mulberry School for Girls, in Tower Hamlets, has achieved a good reputation with its predominantly Bangladeshi parents and pupils for the creation of a school policy which really takes account of the cultural and religious needs of the Bangladeshi community, while stressing the need for high educational achievements (Tomlinson and Hutchison, 1991).

Regrettably there has also been evidence of continuing problems. The insensitive treatment of the parents of Ahmed Ullah, the schoolboy murdered at Burnage High School, Manchester, in 1986, received wide publicity (MacDonald, 1989), and white parental antagonisms to ethnic minority families have been more vocal during the 1980s. During the passage of the Education Reform Bill through Parliament in 1987, opposition peers moved an amendment to remove the duty of local education authorities (LEAs) to comply with parental preference for choice of school if it was believed to be on racial grounds. The amendment was withdrawn after a government minister assured the House of Lords that it was unlikely that white parents would give an openly racist reason for choice of school. In fact, in the opinion of the Commission for Racial Equality, this had already happened, a parent in Cleveland having requested the transfer of her child from a school with a high ethnic population to a school where there was a majority of white children (Commission for Racial Equality, 1989). Other white parents have been using the clauses in the Act requiring religious education to be 'predominantly

Christian' as a way of moving their children away from multi-racial schools. The counsel for the twenty-two Dewsbury parents who in 1987 refused to send their children to a predominantly Asian school claimed that 'the parents have a natural desire that their children should be educated in a traditional English and Christian environment' (Naylor, 1988). The social context in which teachers find themselves, therefore, is not conducive to breaking down stereotypes of minority parents as likely to pose problems for schools.

CONTINUED STEREOTYPING

Teachers, despite some improvements in their education and training courses, continue to have difficulty informing themselves about the lives and backgrounds of ethnic minority parents and continue to resort to stereotyped beliefs about ethnic minority homes. From the 1960s much literature produced about ethnic minorities was simplistic and patronising and often took a static view of culture – customs and traditions brought by migrants were assumed to be unchanging, and dress, diet, religion and language became problems to be solved rather than attributes to be respected. Although the literature 'about' minorities has become more realistic – particularly now that ethnic minority researchers and writers are involved (see Bhachu, 1985; Gilroy, 1987) – teachers find difficulty in appreciating the daily struggle many ethnic minority parents face in living in Britain, or the courage and dignity which they display in the face of racial antagonisms. Many ethnic minority parents still find it shocking to realise the extent of racial hostility, cultural ignorance and stereotyped beliefs exhibited by ordinary people – including some teachers.

Most teachers in urban schools do not, in any case, live among their pupils and those in 'white' schools still obtain much of their information about ethnic minorities from the media. Even teachers in multi-racial schools receive little guidance on contact and communication with ethnic minority parents and this encourages a stereotyping of the parents which it is not easy to eradicate. One stereotyped belief which persists is that ethnic minority parents are 'just like' white working-class parents apart from colour and customs. This can create a double-disadvantage for ethnic minority parents as there is a well-documented history of negative teacher stereotyping of working-class parents (Roberts, 1984), and many teachers have come to believe that school

influences are minimal when set against the perceived disadvantages of a working-class and an ethnic minority background.

Khan (1980) has pointed out that ignorance of other cultures
and ways of life can lead to 'elaborate structures of myth-making'
and she showed how popular stereotypes of Muslim parental treatment of girls and of Afro-Caribbean family structures encouraged
teachers to think of ethnic minority families as automatically creating 'problems'. Recent research by Brar (1991) has demonstrated
that stereotyped ideas of ethnic minority families and communities continue to be held and can prevent genuine contacts
between homes and schools. His work was particularly concerned
to demonstrate how stereotypes are constructed and reinforced.
Knowledge of the 'black community' by teachers in schools in
Handsworth, Birmingham, is still, he found, largely based on
'common sense knowledge and racist media distortion' (p. 33).
The Handsworth community is presumed to be all-black, all
working-class and often all male, and teachers continue to stereotype parents as uninterested in their children's education and
perpetuate a blame-the-parents syndrome which 'has often been
the excuse for schools to sit back and avoid developing school-
community consultation' (p. 34).

Even in schools where there is more knowledge of the variety of
ethnic minority communities – their different socio-economic and
housing conditions and their linguistic, cultural and religious
backgrounds – simple stereotyping still persists, which inhibits
open teacher–parent contact and consultation.

ASSIMILATIONIST AND NATIONALIST VIEWS

One reason for the continued willingness to stereotype ethnic
minority communities and parents is that there has been, over the
past thirty years, an enduring commitment in education to assimilationist views, overlaid more recently by nationalist beliefs which
attempt to exclude ethnic minorities from being part of a 'British
national identity' (Gilroy, 1987; Tomlinson, 1990). During the
1960s the idea that pupils should forget their own languages and
cultures and assimilate into the majority society seemed right and
proper to many teachers. This notion tied in with liberal views that
in order to provide equal opportunities all children should be
treated as if they were 'the same'. However, assimilationist beliefs
rapidly became a way of absolving teachers from learning about

the backgrounds and lives of ethnic minorities or making educational changes and adaptations. Honeyford, the former Bradford headteacher who became a *cause célèbre* in the mid-1980s (see Halstead, 1989), articulated a view still very common in education at the present time, even among younger teachers, that 'some teachers would argue that the responsibility for the adaptation and adjustment to settling into a new country lies entirely with those who have come to settle (Honeyford, 1982).

The arguments against crude notions of assimilation have been well presented by Dench (1986). He has pointed out that, on the one hand, ethnic minorities are urged that the most appropriate way for them to achieve equality of opportunity and acceptance into the nation is to give up adherence to cultures, languages, customs and values, and regard themselves as 'British'. But at the same time the white majority – which includes parents and teachers – remains hostile to ethnic minorities and denies them entry into the idea of the 'nation'. Assimilation is impossible in a society in which the majority culture includes political and cultural beliefs in white superiority and condones racial discrimination, harassment and cultural ignorance. As a further twist to beliefs in assimilation, ethnic minorities can be blamed for their own intransigence if they do exhibit a desire to hold on to their own cultures and languages while at the same time seeking entry to the national identity and to equal citizenship.

During the 1980s a nationalistic backlash, following the disturbances in inner cities in 1981 and 1985, led to the use of militaristic and patriotic metaphors of war to describe immigrant minorities.

> The enemy within, the unarmed invasion, alien encampments, new commonwealth occupations, have all been used to describe the black presence.
>
> (Gilroy, 1987: 45)

In education, a growing antagonism to the development of the kind of plural democratic society envisaged by the Swann Committee (Swann Report, 1985) was evident from the mid-1980s. A former Minister of State for Education asserted that:

> There is a genuine and not dishonourable fear that British values and traditions – the very stuff of school education – are likely to be put at risk if too much allowance is made for the cultural backgrounds and attitudes of ethnic minorities.
>
> (Patten, 1986)

This kind of statement was not likely to make ethnic minority parents feel that they were taken seriously as equal partners in an education system that was beginning to examine its values and its traditions. Nor were such parents likely to feel that consultation had much value when, as happened in Berkshire LEA in 1987, the council attempted to rescind a policy on Education for Racial Equality which had been produced after discussion with a large number of parental and other groups – on the grounds that Berkshire was 'in danger of losing its British heritage, background and national pride' (Berkshire, 1987). Given the lack of positive direction by politicians and policy-makers, many teachers, especially those unfamiliar with the issues, have continued to regard ethnic minority families as problematic, and find difficulty in treating them as equal partners.

BANGLADESHI PARENTS IN TOWER HAMLETS

Research during the 1980s focused more on specific groups of ethnic minority parents, particularly on Afro-Caribbean parents who have continued to be very critical of the education offered to their children. There has been little specific inquiry into Bangladeshi parents' views of education or their contacts with schools, although a number of studies of the educational achievements of ethnic minority pupils have noted that pupils of Bangladeshi origin achieve less well than most other ethnic minority pupils, especially in gaining school-leaving qualifications (Home Affairs Committee, 1987; Inner London Education Authority, 1990). A project in Hertfordshire, in which Bengali families settled in the area were interviewed, concluded that the achievement of their children could be understood in terms of the gap between the educational needs of the community and the provision they were offered. Parents were offered little basic information about schools, there were few strategies to involve parents in schooling and there was a tendency for teachers to 'blame' the community, marginalise pupils and have low expectations (Murshid, 1990). In Tower Hamlets, London, a 1985 study of Bangladeshi mothers found that they had positive attitudes towards education, but schools had few strategies for home–school contacts and communication (Hutchison and Vaarlem, 1985). In 1990 the Advisory Centre for Education (ACE), at that time located in the Borough of Tower Hamlets (which in April 1990 took over the education service from the Inner London Education Authority (ILEA)) commissioned a small research project exploring the views of Bangladeshi parents about their children's education, their levels of knowledge about schooling and the extent of contact and involvement (Tomlinson and Hutchison, 1991). ACE took the view that since government encouragement of parental 'choice' and involvement had become so well-publicised, it was important that no group of parents should be left in a position where they could not become active partners in the education process.

The study, described below, illustrates vividly some of the continued problems ethnic minority parents face in making contact with schools in terms that are meaningful to them – even with schools that have attempted to develop home–school links.

Fifty-three sets of Bangladeshi parents were interviewed in their homes by a Bengali-speaking interviewer between January and March 1990, addresses having been obtained from two schools – one primary, one secondary – which had reputations for good home–school relations. Ten of the families had had a child 'out-of-school' at some point, because of insufficient school places, a situation which had persisted during the 1980s and for which legal remedy had been sought. A request for a judicial review of the 'out-of-school' issue was turned down in 1990 by Lord Justice Woolf who gave the extraordinary judgement that the duty of an education authority to provide sufficient school places under the 1944 Education Act was 'not absolute' (*Ali and Murshid* v. *The Inner London Education Authority*, 14 February 1990).

The Borough of Tower Hamlets ranks high on most indices of poverty and deprivation despite Docklands development. There is a large amount of sub-standard housing, numbers of homeless families and high unemployment. There was a rapid growth in the Bangladeshi population during the 1980s, most heads of households being in semi-skilled or unskilled work. In 1987 forty-four per cent of Tower Hamlets pupils spoke a language other than English in the home – the majority speaking Bengali/Sylheti. Particular educational problems during the 1980s included a school place shortage, a teacher shortage, low educational achievements, a low staying-on rate, and racial harassment of ethnic minority families, including harassment of parents taking children to school. Education officials tended to regard Bangladeshi parents in a somewhat negative light – as creating problems because of large families, disadvantaged circumstances and lack of

English, and indeed the circumstances of the families in the research appeared to confirm this picture. All the families interviewed had three or more children, twenty-nine having five or more, and their accommodation was distinctly overcrowded. A third of mothers and a fifth of fathers had had no schooling at all and were unable to read and write English, and thirty-two per cent of fathers were unemployed – the rest were working in semi-skilled or unskilled jobs or were self-employed. However, all this did not generate a lack of interest in education, or low aspirations. Some of the families were prepared to be very critical of the education system and they had a lively awareness of the disadvantaged nature of their circumstances. They resented stereotypes about their ways of life and attitudes to children and to education.

Size of families – connected to immigration laws which often kept families apart until the later 1970s – are a problem in that schools assume that parents will be dealing with one or two schools at the most. Tower Hamlets parents often have children at four or more schools, sometimes across the primary, secondary and even tertiary divide. To become involved with several schools at once poses especial difficulties. One teacher, who complained that a mother brought her children to school late, did not realise that the mother was delivering children to three schools. The researchers on this project explored another stereotype of ethnic minority homes held by teachers, which Brar also found in his Handsworth study, that 'the black home is deprived of books'. In the homes visited in Tower Hamlets eighty-five per cent had books and forty-three per cent of mothers said that they read books regularly – either in English or Bengali. A wide variety of books were noted: books in both English and Bengali, story books, novels, text-books, encyclopaedias, dictionaries, religious books (every home had a Quran). 'Islamic books, Bengali and English history books, physics, chemistry, biology and general science books, Arabic texts, children's comics, counting and spelling books, study books, library books and books from school' were found in the homes (Tomlinson and Hutchison, 1991).

SOME CONCLUSIONS FROM THE TOWER HAMLETS STUDY

The study suggested that Bangladeshi parental levels of knowledge about education and their children's schooling is inadequate despite high levels of parental intent and aspiration. Knowledge about education was certainly not sufficient to enable parents to exercise their rights and responsibilities as envisaged by new legislation. Contact with schools was on a formal level and there was little informal day-to-day parental involvement. Teachers' views of themselves as professionals, with parents as clients rather than partners, were very much in evidence. For example, teachers were on occasion rather patronising to parents who came to 'help' in the classroom – one teacher joking that her helper could never arrive on time. Even with 'good' schools which attempted to encourage contact, the information passed to parents was limited and insufficient, especially given that ethnic minority parents have not passed through the education system and often needed more information than indigenous parents. There was also a mismatch between parents' and teachers' views of schooling in several important respects – notably over the levels of English competence of the children, whether teachers were accurately informing parents about their children's achievements, the requirements of the 1988 Education Reform Act, and whether teachers respected Bengali culture and religion or displayed ignorance and stereotyping.

The study confirmed that Bangladeshi parents had specific problems related to their socio-economic position, migrant status, and racial and cultural differences – racial attacks are common in Tower Hamlets – and that the problems do affect the education of their children. Parents certainly could not afford to subsidise schools by paying for 'extras' and many families spent a large part of the day delivering and collecting children from school. Lack of English hampered home–school contacts and few teachers had attempted to learn Bengali. Schools recognised that language was a major barrier but had few strategies to overcome the problem. Interestingly, most parents preferred written letters home to be either in English or in English and Bengali. Parents, who had no personal experience of schooling in England, often did not appreciate the high levels of language competence pupils needed in order to function across the curriculum at all levels and, although the acquisition of English was regarded as crucial, there was a mismatch between the schools' views that the children had low levels of English and parental views. One father was so pleased that his daughter could interpret his income-tax form, that he never inquired into her GCSE English performance!

The majority of parents had visited their children's schools, usually to see teachers rather than for social or other events, (few at the secondary school attended the annual meeting to hear the governors' report) and all the parents found the teachers to be 'helpful'. However they did not think that teachers gave the levels of information they wanted about their children's progress. There was limited involvement in classroom activity or on school outings: only four out of sixty parents had helped in primary classrooms.

Although most Tower Hamlets schools have home–school reading schemes the reasons for this were not well understood, some parents feeling they were being delegated a responsibility which belonged to the school, or not feeling confident in their ability to help. Only forty per cent of fathers and fifty per cent of mothers helped with reading at home, and mothers often interpreted 'helping' as keeping other children quiet.

Nearly twenty months after the 1988 Education Reform Act came into operation ninety per cent of mothers and forty per cent of fathers had not heard of the reforms and had only a hazy notion about the national curriculum and testing arrangements. Parents were in favour of regular testing but as a way to assist their children's learning, rather than to criticise teachers and schools. Parents were all in favour of homework, were less likely than in the mid-1980s to send their children to mosque school after regular school, and were not in favour of separate Islamic schools, providing that state schools adapted. The parents of secondary school girls were very appreciative that the school provided an appropriate uniform, a prayer room and halal meat, and offered Bengali and Islamic studies. The parents were in favour of regular schooling for both sexes until after the age of sixteen, and stereotypes of Muslim girls only being prepared for marriage were not supported. Academic and work qualifications were seen as the goal of education, and parents also wanted their children prepared for adulthood as moral beings, taught self-discipline and to be 'of use to the community'. In sum, working-class Bengali parents, often with little English, had an interest in education and a sophistication in their desires for their children which teachers did not credit them with.

PARENT GOVERNORS

The 1988 Education Reform Act equalised representation on governing bodies of local authority representatives and parents, and allowed for the co-option of governors from the community.

The Act greatly increased the powers and duties of governors, especially concerning the curriculum and finance. Governors also have particular responsibilities, such as deciding which documents going to parents should be translated into other languages, and presenting an annual report to all parents. There is an expectation, but no requirement, that parent-governors will make an effort to communicate with other parents. There is a London-based Association of Black Governors which offers some training for members, but a recent national survey of ethnic-minority school governors found that their training was not a priority in local authorities (National Consumer Council, 1990).

Given that membership of a governing body is a major way to participate in school decision-making and to discuss school matters at the level of 'equals' it would seem very important that the governing body of a school reflects the community it serves, and that wherever possible governing bodies should include representatives from ethnic minority groups. However, a survey carried out by the Inner London Education Authority (1989) found that ethnic minorities were severely underrepresented among school governors, and a survey in the following year by the National Consumer Council (NCC) and Action for Governor Information and Training (AGIT) found that 'in areas where there is a concentration of minority ethnic groups, school governing bodies tend to be unrepresentative' (National Consumer Council, 1990). The NCC survey found that fewer than half of all LEAs were taking positive action to recruit ethnic minority community parents, and less than a third were developing training programmes designed to meet the needs of ethnic minority governors. However, the majority of LEAs had made some attempt to make links with ethnic minority community organisations. In the Tower Hamlets research reported above four parent-governors were interviewed. The parent-governors did have a higher level of knowledge and awareness of educational issues than other parents and took their duties very seriously. It would appear that ethnic minority parent-governors are a potential link between homes and schools not fully developed at the moment. The governors interviewed wanted to be more involved with academic and pastoral affairs, asked for more accountability from teachers, and wanted to help other parents and the whole community to be more involved in education.

CONCLUSION

It is relatively easy to point out problems in home–school relations, and more difficult to make positive suggestions to improve parental knowledge about schools and to encourage closer home–school contacts and involvement. This chapter has suggested that the history of relationships between schools and ethnic minority parents over the past thirty years, set within a society still marked by racial and cultural antagonisms, makes it more difficult to develop positive home–school contacts and involvement than with indigenous parents. There is evidence that teachers are still not well-informed about the lives, backgrounds, expectations and desires of ethnic minority parents and are still willing to stereotype such families as 'problems'. Ethnic minority parents are less likely than white parents to be involved in day-to-day school activities and to be represented on governing bodies. There is still a mismatch between ethnic minority parents' views as to how far schools can raise their children's achievement levels and, in the study reported in this chapter, such parents were not well-informed about new curriculum and assessment arrangements and other educational innovations which were intended to raise achievements. On the positive side, ethnic minority parents, together with other parents, have benefited to some extent from requirements that schools provide more information about the process of schooling, and some urban multi-racial schools have developed more open and sensitive contacts and consultation with ethnic minority families and communities. The recommendations made below to improve relations and bring ethnic minority homes and schools closer together are concerned with teacher professionalism, teacher education, and the statutory requirement for every school to have a Home–School Association.

- Teacher concepts of their professionalism should include a willingness to consult with, offer information to, and involve all parents, but especially ethnic minority parents, in the process of schooling, on a basis of equality. This will require an enormous change of attitude. It was noted at the beginning of this chapter that teachers are currently urged to think of parents as clients, consumers and critics rather than as equal partners.
- Teacher education at both initial and in-service level should include for all teachers, wherever they work or plan to work, a

course in which they learn something about their ethnic minority fellow-citizens and become aware of the dangers of stereotyping pupils, parents and communities.

* A new statutory framework should be developed by which all parents are given a voice in the decision-making process in schools. All schools should be required to create a Home–School Association of which all parents are automatically members with a right to be consulted on educational matters.

* The Home–School Association would exist to discuss matters relating to children's learning, progress and development. It would be a forum for teachers to pass on knowledge and information about schooling to parents, and for parents to pass on information on home learning and home background to teachers. The associations would debate matters relating to the curriculum, assessment, teaching methods, progress and achievement. Parents would not be expected to defer to teachers or heads, and the schools would be open to dialogue with all parents, whatever their socio-economic, cultural or linguistic background. Home–School Associations would liaise with governing bodies but would be the statutory vehicle for bringing homes and schools closer together (see Tomlinson, 1991).

* More should be done to encourage those from ethnic minorities to qualify and train as teachers.

Over the past thirty years, voluntary efforts have not brought ethnic minority homes and schools into the closer relationship that is necessary if their children are to be offered a fair and equal education in a system that will need, in the future, to respect and involve all parents much more fully.

A new statutory framework is now needed to bring about a situation in which ethnic minority parents can be equal partners in the education of their children.

REFERENCES

Ali and Murshid v *The Inner London Education Authority,* London, 14 February 1990.

Berkshire (1987) *Multicultural Education Policy Guidelines,* Slough: Berkshire County Council.

Bhachu, P. (1985) *Twice Migrants,* London: Tavistock.

Brar, H.S. (1991) 'Teaching, Professionalism, and Home–School Links', *Multicultural Teaching* 9(1): 32–5.

Commission for Racial Equality (1989) *Racial Segregation in Education: Report of a Formal Investigation into Cleveland Education Authority*, London: Commission for Racial Equality.

Dench, G. (1986) *Minorities in an Open Society: Prisoners of Ambivalence*, London: Routledge.

Education Act 1944, London: HMSO.

Education Act 1980, London: HMSO.

Education Act (No. 2) 1986, London: HMSO.

Education Reform Act 1988, London: HMSO.

Gilroy, P. (1987) *There Ain't No Black in the Union Jack*, London: Hutchinson.

Halstead, M. (1989) *Education, Justice and Cultural Diversity*, Lewes: Falmer.

Home Affairs Committee (1987) *Bangladeshis in Britain*, London: HMSO.

Home–School Contract of Partnership Newsletter (1991) 3 (Summer).

Honeyford, R. (1982) 'Multi-racial Myths', *Times Educational Supplement*, 19 November.

Hutchison, S. and Vaarlem, A. (1985) *Bangladeshi Mothers' Views of Schooling in Tower Hamlets*, London: Inner London Education Authority.

Inner London Education Authority (1989) *Ethnic Minority Parent Governors*, London: Inner London Education Authority.

Inner London Education Authority (1990) *Differences in Examination Performance*, London: Inner London Education Authority.

Khan, V. (1980) *Minority Families in Britain: Support and Stress*, London: Tavistock.

MacDonald, I. (1989) *Murder in the Playground*, Manchester: Longright Press.

Murshid, T. (1990) 'Needs Perceptions and Provision: The Problem of Achievement among Bengali (Sylheti) Pupils', *Multicultural Teaching* 8(3): 12–16.

National Consumer Council (1990) *Minority Ethnic Communities and School Governing Bodies*, London: National Consumer Council.

Naylor, F. (1988) 'Political Lessons of Dewsbury', *The Independent*, 22 December.

Parker-Jenkins, M. (1991) 'Muslim Matters: The Educational Needs of the Muslim Child', *New Community* 17(4): 569–82.

Patten, C. (1986) Address to HMI Conference, Buxton.

Rampton Report (1981) *West Indian Children in Our Schools*, Department of Education and Science, London: HMSO.

Rex, J. and Tomlinson, S. (1979) *Colonial Immigrants in a British City*, London: Routledge.

Roberts, K. (1984) *School Leavers and Their Prospects*, Milton Keynes: Open University Press.

Smith, D. and Tomlinson, S. (1989) *The School Effect: A Study of Multi-racial Comprehensives*, London: Policy Studies Institute.

Swann Report (1985) *Education for All*, Department of Education and Science, London: HMSO.

Tomlinson, S. (1984) *Home and School in Multi-cultural Britain*, London: Batsford.

Tomlinson, S. (1985) 'The Black Education Movement', in Arnot, M. (ed.) *Race and Gender*, Milton Keynes: Open University Press.

Tomlinson, S. (1990) *Multicultural Education in White Schools*, London: Batsford.

Tomlinson, S. (1991) *Home–School Partnerships* (Education and Training Paper No. 7), London: Institute for Public Policy Research.

Tomlinson, S. and Hutchison, S. (1991) *Bangladeshi Parents and Education in Tower Hamlets*, London: Advisory Centre for Education.

Townsend, H.E.R. and Brittan, E. (1972) *Organisation in Multiracial Schools*, Slough: NFER-Nelson.

Venning, P. (1983) 'Menacing Warning Sent to Haringey Heads over Exams', *Times Educational Supplement*, 11 February.

Chapter 10

Parents and schools
What role for education authorities?

Charles Raab

Partnership, and the notion of parents as partners, figure in this book as key elements in the analysis of current developments in the education systems of England and Wales and of Scotland. Such focusing reflects the broader idiom of public debate within circles of policy-making and practice where the rights, responsibilities, expectations, resources and purposes of partnership are negotiated and arbitrated. Converting the public idiom into the coinage of analysis serves to disengage the concepts from their role in policy debates and to reposition them within discourses that cast light on events, rather than add strength to contending interests within political arenas.

This chapter, in part, steps back from events in order to develop some conceptual themes that may enable a fresh look to be taken at what has sometimes become a fairly unproductive political argument about relationships and powers in a public system like education and, in particular, about the role of local education authorities (LEAs) in the reformed education systems of Britain. It attempts to bring some considerations from the wider field of policy studies to bear upon the relatively closed dialogue of educational policy and practice. Referring to some recent research, much of which is preliminary, the chapter addresses the question of the place of LEAs, one of the participants in a now-discredited partnership, in the new relationships that are being forged under the aegis of government policies that have been implanted since the 1970s.

PARTNERSHIP AND ITS TRANSFORMATION

A repositioning of terms is necessary because, as Golby notes in Chapter 5, partnership is 'largely an honorific term'. Moreover, as has been argued elsewhere (McPherson and Raab, 1988; Raab, 1992), it has had a strongly rhetorical flavour, asserting the claims and counter-claims of groups in political conflict. It celebrates as well as describes relationships in referring to a division and sharing of power and authority. But the relationship so described and valued is not one simply between decision-maker and implementer, because the implementer must be able to influence the decision as well as pursue some aims autonomously, within an overall agreement. In addition, 'partnership' is part of the language of a game in the policy process, in which, for example, one of the parties might invoke the term in order to signal to the other that it should not be treated as a mere agent of the other's will, or to serve notice that there are mutual responsibilities that may be endangered through conflict.

Dictionaries are not always good sources for the meaning of concepts. The *Shorter Oxford English Dictionary* says that a partner 'has a share or part with another or others', or 'is associated in any function, act, or course of action'; 'partnership' it gives as the 'fact or condition of being a partner'. Although this does not get us very far, it serves as a reminder of how far additional assumptions have accreted to this stripped-down definition. However, it is not clear why the notion of equality, in particular, has crept into some interpretations of partnership in the field of education and elsewhere, in terms of which meaning an imbalance of power or influence is taken to violate the spirit of partnership. Business partnerships and alliances in international relations, for example, do not necessarily indicate equality except in certain limited terms of formal status. Inequality amongst partners is an important characteristic for explanations of action, and also for the practical politics of relationships, but it seems more useful as a variable rather than as part of a definition.

Partnership denotes not only formal powers and obligations, but also interaction. Outcomes are not just the aggregated result of separate performances, but also reflect joint and articulated contributions by partners whose linkages and exchanges may nevertheless vary in their characteristics. Trust is important to partnership, although problems of trusting and trustworthiness may pervade the conditions of exchange. Here too, there are many variables in the nuances and characteristics of partnerships, such as the tightness or looseness of the linkages and interactions amongst the partners, the density, frequency and exclusivity of the network of relationships, and the degree of mutual dependence upon each other's performance (Raab, 1992).

Whatever these complications and ambiguities may be, the partnership to which this chapter mainly refers is not the horizontal one between parents and schools at the same level, but the vertical one linking participants at different levels into a system of policy-making and implementation. Macbeth (1990) argues that there is very wide latitude available for school boards in Scotland to develop their own modes and extent of participation; the same is true of governing bodies in England and Wales. These relations between parents and schools, however, are strongly affected by the kinds of relations that occur vertically, for parents' roles in schooling are shaped by central government legislation and by local authority implementation as well as by local policy tendencies. All of these establish not only the statutory and financial framework within which parent–school partnership relations of various kinds may occur, but also many of the external expectations about the scope and content of these interactions.

The traditional partnership in education was a fragile one in which trust was often at a premium and in which consensus was perhaps more specious than real, as Kogan (1987) claims. It embraced central and local government, reflecting the broader and equally rhetorical use of the term in central–local relations generally. In particular, it is the central education departments and the LEAs to whom 'partnership' has often been imputed, but it has also included teachers, who campaigned hard to achieve the status of partner and who complain when they are not so treated. A complicating factor is that there are three senses in which teachers may be partners with central and local government: as teachers whose individual or collective work constitutes an implementation of policy decided elsewhere; as individuals whose classroom practice, in effect, becomes policy; and as collective actors in organisations and in policy networks that represent a professional interest in the policy process.

The empowerment of parents and the encouragement of their participation in school decision-making has been driven in large part by government's revulsion against the vertical partnership and its supposed dominance by a closed educational world of professional and bureaucratic interests operating in central government, in LEAs and in the schools. This partnership was held to have kept the influence of parents, politicians and wider industrial and economic interests at bay, to the detriment of schooling and the national interest alike. Political initiatives for comprehensive education invaded the partnership and exacerbated relations between central and local levels in the 1960s. Dissatisfaction about 'standards' gathered momentum in the 1970s and first came to a head under the auspices of a Labour government. Although the voices of discontent with the education system were muted in Scotland, in England and Wales the political temperature of education rose sharply. Central government, especially under the Conservatives, became politically more assertive in the education field and impacted strongly upon whatever partnership there may have been.

Over a number of years, trust in professionals' judgement has been replaced by performance-measurement in accordance with finely gradated criteria, and new external forms of accountability have been instituted. Education departments at central and local levels now have an enhanced role in monitoring and inspecting the performance of schools, and in developing the criteria and information systems that are necessary for this to be done. This points in the direction of 'steering at a distance' and other sophisticated forms of control (Bogason 1991; Kickert, 1991), in which information about performance plays an important role, but their effectiveness and reliability under conditions of political or interest conflict and mistrust leave them open to scepticism. Much depends upon whether the control systems are imposed from the top, in which case the 'game' at the middle or the bottom will be to outsmart and deceive the higher levels (the antithesis of 'partnership'), or are genuinely negotiated and in some sense self-imposed.

The centralisation of power on which government has embarked may prove to be a Pyrrhic victory if its use as a lever for educational change is inhibited by the recalcitrance and non-compliance of those upon whom central government greatly depends. There is much in the history of the more-centralised Scottish system that points to the conclusion that government cannot go it alone (McPherson and Raab, 1988). It can only implement its policies through exchanges of resources in inter-organisational relationships and networks that are reasonably committed and trustworthy (Raab, 1992; Rhodes, 1988; Scharpf, 1978). It must work hard to create and maintain such interdependent implementation structures, and it cannot always, if ever, choose those with whom it is interdependent. Some are thrust upon it like obnoxious fellow-passengers on a cruise ship, and cannot be thrown overboard with impunity. Government may, however, seek to reduce their opportunities for obstruction, or reduce its degree of dependence upon them. It may also try to constrict their autonomy and lock them into systems and roles designed by government and operating to government's advantage, such as monitoring systems. None of this is easily accomplished, but it is being attempted.

These developments must be seen in the context of the broader rupture of partnership assumptions concerning the position of local government that has occurred within the lifetime of the Conservative government of the 1980s and early 1990s. This is not the place to rehearse the political and financial battles of those years, during which central government restructured relationships across many service functions of the state and reduced local government's control (Hampton, 1991). The attack on the position of local government is best seen as a general phenomenon occurring far more widely than the education service itself. Kean (1991) points out that it was not only the specific education legislation that impacted on the education service, but also the overall constraints that were imposed on local authorities' capital expenditure and other financial arrangements. In addition, legislation that inaugurated competitive tendering and other innovations had the effect of eroding local authorities' role even further.

In many respects the upsetting of traditional relationships in education has been cut from the same cloth as these developments. This was woven from the discrediting of professionals and of administrators, mainly but not exclusively at the local level; from hostility to the policies that they had implanted over a long period of time; and from a revulsion against increasing public expenditure upon services. The initiative in the making and implementation of policy was wrested from the hands of the entrenched policy communities that had stretched across levels of government and institutional sites of practice in each field, and was transferred to other players: to government ministers, to the laity, and to governmental organisations and outside interests that had not been prominently involved before. An important thread in the weave was the relocation of decision-making to newly legitimated markets, such that 'policy', in effect, is potentially merely the aggregated result of individual market choices for which no one is specifically responsible. In education, for example, the cumulative effects of parental choice of schools and opting-out may achieve the government's desired results in the absence of deliberate decision-making in the customary political arenas. As Ball (1990a) makes clear, however, in this commodification of education the market is anything but a value-neutral instrument.

Nor does government merely abandon the policy pitch to market players, for it retains and even strengthens its central powers of determination above and beyond its licensing of stall-holders in the market and its regulation of many of the prices and standards for the items traded there. Decentralisation does not of itself either constitute decontrol or remove implementation from the orbit of central management. Working in part through headteachers and governing bodies or, in Scotland, school boards, decentralisation can only achieve its object if markets work as they are supposed theoretically to work, and if values, interests, energies and behaviour at the periphery are consonant with the qualities and levels that government assumes. Decentralisation cannot amount to a 'hands off' strategy of steering towards goals so long as political or managerial responsibility remains at the top for the achievement of overall ends (Kickert, 1991; Metcalfe, 1991). Government must design the system and its networks such that those decisions that are taken decentrally are within a range that is compatible with the achievement of its own objectives. Such 'macro-management' (Metcalfe, 1991) may mean restricting the scope for autonomous decision at the periphery or, alternatively, getting its partners to want what the centre thinks they ought to want.

Kogan (1987) sums up the new atmosphere as one in which central government quite simply distrusts local authorities to spend money wisely or to pursue acceptable policies, and insists instead on its own prescriptions for change. In England and Wales, legislation in the 1980s embarked upon the restructuring of the vertical partnership in education. This cannot be discussed in any detail in this chapter, but is analysed in many useful sources (Ball, 1990b; Chitty, 1989; Dale, 1989; Flude and Hammer, 1990; Hargreaves and Reynolds, 1989; Maclure, 1988). The 1980 Education Act widened the scope of parental choice of school and enhanced parents' representation on governing bodies (Kogan *et al.*, 1984), as well as required schools to become more accountable by providing more information. The 1986 Education (No. 2) Act went further in the direction of enfranchising parents and of promoting greater accountability of schools. It increased considerably the representation of parents and co-opted members of the local community on governing bodies, and reduced that of the LEA. It gave greater powers to governing bodies and placed new duties upon them to report to parents. A crucial development was government's reliance on the Manpower Services Commission (MSC), as it was then called, to develop programmes and disburse vast financial resources in the field of training and vocational education. Another blow was struck against LEAs' discretion to spend according to their own priorities by the growth of specific grants, although that discretion was always limited by the commitment of resources to paying teachers' salaries and maintaining buildings.

But it was the 1988 Education Reform Act (ERA) that envisaged the most decisive shift in the distribution of power and responsibility in education since 1944. If it were fully implemented, it would radically relocate education within the parameters of market and consumer choice, and would represent the eclipse of professional and bureaucratic control over schooling in favour of politicians, parents and business interests. Its main provisions instigating this shift are those for a national curriculum, parental choice, devolved school budgets under the control of school governing bodies, grant-maintained status, City Technology Colleges, and the removal of polytechnics and advanced further-education colleges from local authority control. The powerful political and organisational thrust of this legislation is, arguably, to strengthen central government, although the government itself claims that its aim is to empower and to enfranchise parents, governing bodies and thus the schools themselves. Either way, and especially both, it is the power of the local level that looks like being redistributed, casting doubt upon the ability of LEAs to engage as partners with central government and with schools or teachers.

The extent to which strong state control is ideologically and practically compatible with a dispersal of power to the periphery of the public sector and to the vagaries of market choice is discussed elsewhere (for example, Ball, 1990b; Raab, forthcoming; Whitty, 1990). But most observers agree that the effect of the ERA, if not its very intention, is to undermine much of the LEAs' control and responsibility and, some would say, to deprive them of their rationale. They may find themselves increasingly redundant or at least shorn of powers, and their services destabilised, as envisaged by Simon (1988) and by Walton (1988). Writing when the ERA was not yet on the Statute Book, Walton, then Sheffield's Chief Education Officer, estimated the life-expectancy of local government at much less than twenty years. However, as will be considered below, LEAs are intended to retain an important strategic role in relation to planning and managing education, although the reality of this expectation remains to be seen. In practice, a complex pattern may emerge in which both centralising and decentralising tendencies may in fact result along different dimensions, at the expense of the local authorities, but probably not with fatal consequences. Prognoses of doom are only plausible on a reading of the policy process that takes central government's legislation and declarations of intent as *faits accomplis* on the ground. But government is neither omnipotent nor omniscient, and the proof of the pudding is in the implementation, not the formation, of policy. Moreover, even if government policy were taken at face value, it would by no means indicate the utter enfeeblement of local authorities and LEAs; those voices who have advocated that within Conservative government circles have been marginalised. But if policies were implemented with a reasonable degree of 'success', in the eyes of central government, what role would be left for the local education authorities? And what would become of 'partnership'?

THE PLACE OF THE EDUCATION AUTHORITIES

It would be risky to claim any certainty for answers to these questions, and clarity will only be possible given the passage of time and the conduct of research. Moreover, there is no reason to expect a uniform settlement across the country; even under the old partnership, LEAs differed in the way they 'partnered' central government. However, there is already a variety of expectations based upon different readings of the Acts and of the situation. Kean's (1991) view is that, in many local services, councils are forced to act as implementers of government legislation and not as political strategic planners. The local authority, she argues, is seen as a board of managing directors who seek tenders, issue contracts, and monitor performance; its only strategic role is to balance the books. Ranson's (1990: 13) version of this is that the LEA loses much of its status and authority under the ERA: 'Its former powers and responsibilities are largely dissolved or redistributed . . . the LEA may no longer be a tier of government but be limited to efficient implementation of national plans or accurate reading of market trends.'

On the other hand, a role that is substantially larger than that is envisaged for local authorities by Ranson himself and by other commentators or proponents of the new order. Ranson's scenario will be dealt with later, because it touches upon wider considerations to be discussed more fully at that point. But it may be premature to pronounce local authorities dead in the field of education, or indeed in other services. They may be wounded but they are still walking and are likely to recover, although they will have to adjust to a new level of activity. Whilst their room for manoeuvre is severely circumscribed by the requirements of new legislation, some leverage remains for LEAs to exercise in ways that may influence the education provided by schools and the development of the horizontal partnership between schools and parents. Nor, incidentally, should it be assumed that the laity can implement new education policies at school level without the support and commitment of the ostensibly despised professionals in schools and in LEAs; an ironic conclusion, as Thomas (1990) observes.

Ron Wallace's (1990: 226) view is that local government has both lost and gained under recent legislation: 'the main losses are administrative and financial. The main gains are curricular and concerned with the promotion and monitoring of quality.' Against the pessimists, Wallace, an LEA Chief Adviser and former teacher and headteacher, considers that some of the lost administrative powers were illusory and that changes will not be so great. One of the fears that LEAs had about the provision of the 1988 Act that allows schools to leave local-authority control and become grant-maintained (GM) with funds directly from central government, was that it would severely restrict the ability of LEAs to plan the provision of school places, including the closing of some schools, in a context of falling school rolls and surplus capacity that was uneconomic to maintain. There has been no rush of schools towards GM status; the numbers that have actually opted out of local authority control are barely into treble figures at the start of 1992, although many more (but still fewer than two per cent of all maintained schools) have taken steps to do so. Research reported by Halpin et al., (1991) shows that more than half of the GM schools have opted out in order to avoid closure or redesignation by the LEA, but Wallace argues that closures have never been easy and depend heavily upon national and local political considerations.

Halpin *et al.* reveal a mixed picture across LEAs. Most LEAs contain at least one school that wishes GM status, and some have several such; the disturbance caused to LEA planning has varied considerably and has not always been great overall. Whilst they observe that in some instances even one school's decision to opt out can throw a spanner in the works if it is a school that is crucial to the scheme of things, their evidence leads them to support Wallace's point about the relative difficulty of effecting closures before and after the 1988 Act. They go on to report that the LEAs in their study find it expedient to develop good working relations with GM schools, including selling them services and paying them for the community use of their physical facilities. In concluding that most LEAs' antipathy to opting-out is likely to be modified as LEAs adjust strategically to their reduced powers and perhaps consolidate their influence within a local mixed system of GM and LEA schools, they quote an LEA official who envisaged the LEA 'at the centre but not at the top' of this system (Halpin *et al.*, 1991: 421). But they point out the 'world of difference between being influential, providing information and regulating quality and developing and implementing your own policy' (p. 422).

On the other hand, Wallace takes a different view in anticipating that LEAs may have 'a much more interventionist and influential role in relation to schools . . . than they have previously had' (Wallace, 1990: 231). This is because LEAs play a crucial part in schools' development plans for the national curriculum and for more general functions. Against the conventional wisdom, he sees in these changes 'a significant shift of responsibility from heads and principals to local authorities' (p. 231), although governors, heads and principals have received new powers under the ERA. In exercising this responsibility, LEAs will be acting in large part as the agents, not the partners, of central government, but this still leaves them scope and even some financial resources to promote their own curricular and other policies, and to enjoin these on schools.

The picture painted by this interpretation is that of a new interdependence between the LEA and the school, one in which the freedom and power gained by the institution and its parents and governing body is less, and the influence of the LEA more, than might have been supposed, with central government retaining the upper hand. Wallace says that 'greater parental and professional power in the administrative aspects of running institutions is being balanced by greater control of learning' (Wallace, 1990: 239). Further insights into the interrelationships between LEAs and schools are provided by Mike Wallace (1991). His investigation of the implementation of development plans for schools by LEAs, who are charged with this responsibility, shows how LEAs are able to use the process for promoting not only central government's policies amongst the schools, but also their own as well. These plans are drawn up by schools under LEA direction, and are intended to enable schools to co-ordinate their implementation of central and local policies as well as their own innovations. LEAs can thus pursue their own interest in controlling school development to a high degree, and are not merely the supportive helpmeet of the schools. On the other hand, since the implementation of central and local policies depends upon the co-operation of schools, the latter are able to pursue their own interests within the entire development-plan process in ways that do not necessarily conflict with the externally imposed interests.

As described by Wallace, these reciprocities seem in part to resemble those of the general 'power-dependence' model of inter-governmental relations described by Rhodes (1988), and for which exchange theories might also be relevant (Raab, 1992). In any case, Wallace's research describes the large and even directive role played by LEAs in guiding schools in their development planning, in the subsequent monitoring of schools' performance, and in enabling the LEA to be better informed in order to extract, for example, in-service training resources from the Department of Education and Science (DES) – now the Department for Education (DfE). He considers that 'school development plans may be a key component of evolving LEA policies to establish an influential role with schools in the future' (Wallace, 1991: 391). Yet the LEA may mainly be complying with DES directives in playing its supportive role and, he argues, the LEA's inflexible planning process may unwittingly contribute to schools' interest in controlling their own development at a time of rather feverish and turbulent educational reform. On the basis of this preliminary research, the outcome in terms of LEAs' influence and position between central government and the schools appears to be still indeterminate and negotiable, up to a point. But the judgement of Halpin *et al.* (1991) must be borne in mind, that, even if they are able to reinsert themselves into a position of influence locally, it is unlikely that LEAs will be able to remedy the reproduction of inequalities that opting-out and market choice reinforce.

Another indication of the resilience of LEAs is found in Thomas and Levăcić's (1991) detailed study of DES approval of local management of schools (LMS) schemes. This illustrates how the LEA's ability to control schools through resource-allocation has been curtailed, such that a radical transformation of LEAs' and schools' relative power can be envisaged as a result of the 1988 Act's tendency to centralise in order to decentralise. However, they also conclude that scope remains for LEAs to exercise discretion, and thereby to regain much influence and control, even within the strictures of formula funding; the achievement of central government's aims is not yet guaranteed. In a related article, Thomas (1991) says that, contrary to expectations, LEAs have not lost their individuality and originality in the LMS schemes submitted for DES approval. A similar observation is made by Lee (1990), whose study of LMS schemes found that every LEA has developed its own approach, with a scheme that varies from every other. Lee goes as far as to emphasise that not only administration, but also education policy-making goes on at the local level. 'Despite what many see as an authoritarian and "centrist" government in power, a significant degree of local flexibility was not only allowed for by the legislation but it was positively encouraged' (Lee, 1990: 1). The DES, of course, laid down rules for LEAs to follow, but 'the character of individual schemes reflect[s] the unique interaction of central and local government policy-making processes in each area' (p. 1).

THE EDUCATION AUTHORITY AS 'ENABLER' AND MANAGER

Ranson's vision of a new role for the local authorities was mentioned earlier. He puts it in terms of a 'learning democracy . . . one that listens, enables expression and strives for understanding' (Ranson, 1990: 17), and relates it to a notion of active citizenship and, indeed, of governing bodies as arenas for partnership, not consumer power. This proposal takes the ERA at its word in one sense, that of its 'intention to celebrate more active public choice and accountability' (p. 14), but reverses the thrust of central government's individual-consumerist ethos and revitalises,

...stead, a conception of active citizenship and collective public choice in public domains (Ranson and Stewart, 1989). This turnabout would amount to a 'bottom-up' approach, in which a top-directed hierarchy faces trouble

> as local people organize for action on the problem as they see it, using existing programmes as a resource kit, and feel free to bend the rules of these . . . the important feature is the ability of local officials and private individuals to pool resources in ways that are well suited to a local problem and not foreseen by a central policy maker.
>
> (Bogason, 1991: 198–9)

We may incidentally note that citizenship as an 'idea in good currency' (Schon, 1971) has more recently taken form in the Conservative government's Citizen's Charter (HMSO, 1991), in which the term 'citizen' is appropriated for essentially consumerist purposes, although the charter is designed to promote much of the accountability and service-improvement that citizens, even in Ranson's terms, might come to expect in a democracy.

But Ranson, and Ranson and Stewart, go beyond this to envisage the local authority as the site of improved public learning, participation and accountability. LEAs can do this by serving educational institutions, advising on leadership and progress, and encouraging clear, consistent thinking. They can enable schools to plan; can assist them in setting standards and disseminating good practice; can help them to manage progression between educational stages and to tailor staff development to schools' needs; and can encourage good management. All of this presupposes the involvement of the public. Here 'the role of the LEA is to facilitate public accountability and participation by presenting information, evaluating performance, thereby enabling public discussion about achievement and educational purpose' (Ranson, 1990: 17). In writing about formula funding, Thomas (1991: 84) says that

> the authority's role, once it has shed its authoritarian garb, is to become strategic and supportive, creating policy and model procedures rather than issuing instructions . . . Perhaps the most important role of the LEA is to monitor, evaluate and review the education given.

At this point, the role of the LEA, and the local authority more generally, is set squarely within the framework of another idea in good currency, that of the 'enabling authority'. This notion has figured in academic and practical writing concerned with local government, and has even found its way into the government's proposals for restructuring local government, in which 'local authorities as enablers' (Department of the Environment, 1991, para. 19) are approvingly distinguished from the older conception of local authorities as the main providers of services; they are now seen as setting standards, specifying the work and monitoring performance. The Citizen's Charter shares this view, in saying that local authorities' 'real task' is not the traditional direct provision of services, but

> lies in setting priorities, determining the standards of service . . . and finding the best ways to meet them. By concentrating on these strategic responsibilities they will enable their communities to enjoy higher standards, more choice, better value for money and a greater degree of involvement in the decisions which affect them.
>
> (HMSO, 1991: 34)

Clarke and Stewart (1990: 252) refer to the enabling authority in broad terms as one that 'enables the community to meet its needs and problems', and in narrower terms as 'enabling other organisations to do the work for which the authority is responsible'. Ranson and Stewart write that 'the public domain has to control but also has to facilitate and enable' (Local Government Training Board, 1988: 12), and elaborate a conception of management that fulfils this enablement function (Local Government Training Board, 1988; Ranson and Stewart, 1989).

The theme of enablement is taken further by Brooke (1989, 1991). 'The true enabling authority', he writes, 'will take a synoptic view of the community and its needs. It will assess those needs, plan a strategy, devise action and monitor continuously the movement towards the achievement of community targets' (Brooke, 1991: 529). It will use many different resources and levers to influence other agencies who act in the local field. It will act as leader, broker and co-ordinator, and provide 'a focus for partnership' (p. 529). It will be committed to participatory and representative democracy. As it is less heavily or directly involved in providing services, having devolved these by statutory requirement or otherwise to organisations and agencies at arm's length, the local authority will not only regulate and monitor, but will also try to influence the latter and to 'achieve synergistic solutions' (Brooke, 1989: 59) with agencies whose policies converge with its own. Akin to this argument is Alexander's picture of the local authority at the hub of a loosely linked, local public-sector network of organisation, groups, boards and others that are involved in services, a complex organisational form that has now largely replaced a vertically integrated, hierarchical structure. In these circumstances, the 'new' local authority must manage the effects of fragmentation, and should strive to effect 'community government', which is 'the process of taking the overview of the needs and demands of its area and people and then seeking, by both direct provision and by working through other bodies, to meet the needs and satisfy the demands' (Alexander, 1991: 74). Accountability depends upon the success of the local authority 'in energising the many agencies . . ., monitoring their success . . . and assessing the performance of the services delivered' (pp. 75–6). Stretching the point a bit further, one might envisage such a local authority setting out to alter the networks and the conditions under which its local partners take decisions, such that the local authority can the more successfully achieve its own objectives, in much the same way as central government's ostensible decentralisation to the periphery did not constitute the abandonment of control. But it is open to question how far local authorities in fact have the scope to act in this way, or in the more wide-ranging and creative modes that are suggested by the eloquent evangelists of the 'enabling' approach. It is also open to question how far they would have the political legitimacy to act in this way if they became unelected bodies, as some have proposed.

With specific regard to education, the replacement of detailed control by a focus on major policy issues was envisaged in the Coopers and Lybrand report on LMS and its consequences for LEAs. These consultants did not take the view that the ERA would leave LEAs with little to do, but saw their role in terms of setting the framework for schools, including aims and objectives and the implementation of the curriculum; devising the method of resource-allocation; determining the total level of resources given to schools; monitoring and accountability; and operating sanctions where necessary (Coopers and Lybrand, 1988: 29). A series of reports by the Audit Commission (1988, 1989a, 1989b) have elaborated a number of the themes of enablement and monitoring in encouraging LEAs to reformulate their role under the new legislation. Describing the shifts of power from LEAs upwards to central government, downwards to educational institutions, and outwards to parents, the Audit Commission seeks to reassure that substantial powers as well as responsibilities remain to the LEA, which is 'in short, central to the success of the reform package' (Audit Commission, 1989b: 3). It notes that there is scope for local discretion in the search for a new role, which will combine several approaches: the LEA as leader, partner, planner, provider of information, regulator and banker. Whilst not minimising the effort required in this search and reorientation, the Audit Commission's implication is that LEAs have much to play for, and that the outcome in terms of role and power is not completely determined by legislation. Despite the many duties placed upon LEAs, they are still vested with the responsibility for ensuring that an effective education service is provided, and this may legitimise an activist interpretation of their position. On the other hand, the 1992 Education (Schools) Act provides for a radically restructured, 'privatised' inspection system and for a concomitant redistribution of resources which seem to pose a further threat to LEAs' ability to pursue these ends through their inspection and advisory services, reducing both their leverage over the schools and their ability to support and to guide them. The implications for LEAs were keenly debated between Government and Opposition as the legislation went through its standing-committee stage at the end of 1991.

It is interesting to note that in the past, albeit under very different circumstances and stimulated by very different causes, central government has often cast itself into synoptic, broad-policy roles, once having cleared its decks of responsibility for the minutiae of service-provision that could be left to the local authorities or other bodies. The Scottish Education Department (SED), for example, sought to reach the peaks of policy development and management in the 1960s by shifting routine burdens to new quasi-governmental 'fringe' bodies and to the education authorities (McPherson and Raab, 1988). Its Secretary wanted to devolve to the latter the day-to-day decision-making and trouble-shooting, and to move the SED 'steadily from negative and particular control to positive and general guidance' (Graham, 1965: 302). Griffith's (1966) rough and overlapping classification of types of central department in relation to local authorities included the *laissez-faire*, which interferes little; the *regulatory*, which controls, inspects and enforces standards but does not get closely involved; and the *promotional*, which encourages, advises and helps the local authorities to carry out their functions. One generation on, and moving down the organisational strata to the local authorities and LEAs in relation to executive bodies and to schools, it may be that the concept of the enabling authority in part combines elements of promotion with those of regulation, seeking ways to exert 'positive and general guidance' as well as influence over policies and decisions taken at street level or chalk-face. *Laissez-faire*, if interpreted to mean non-interference with what goes on in basic institutions or in the realm of market choices in education or other local services, does not seem to be a serious option for LEAs in regard to local schools, any more than it is, or has been, for central–local government relations.

A NEW CULTURE FOR PARTNERSHIP?

If there is still scope for partnership, whether vertical or horizontal, it is likely to be one that crystallises around a new paradigm that includes a variety of elements drawn from older systems of hierarchical control, from a new predilection for deregulation and market mechanisms, and from a search for new instruments of governance and management that are adapted from cybernetic and steering models (Dunsire, 1990; Hood, 1983; Kickert, 1991; Metcalfe, 1991). These approaches cannot be elaborated here, but one strong implication is a shift from administration to management, not only in terms of technique but also in terms of culture. In the 1980s and 1990s, there has been a broad movement in British government generally of which the efficiency strategy, decentralisation, performance monitoring, and management information systems are among the main pillars. The cultural revolution that is under way in Whitehall is one in which public management supplants traditional administration (Efficiency Unit, 1988; Metcalfe and Richards, 1990). Such, too, is the explicit ideology behind LMS, whose progenitors call for a new culture and philosophy of the organisation of education (Coopers and Lybrand, 1988).

The implementation of policy is only 'safe' for those in central government and the LEAs who retain policy-making and strategic roles to the extent that a common culture comes to be shared. The mere imposition of external controls by central government upon LEAs, or by LEAs upon their local 'partners' may be effective but costly. Each level may think it preferable if the systems and ethos of management come to legitimise new routines and functions and are self-imposed, or collaboratively adopted, from top to toe. The common culture now being sought is less a philosophy of education than a philosophy of educational management. But if it becomes less a philosophy of management than a mechanical performance of managerial routines in schools and LEAs, then it will have foregone the opportunities for learning, inter-organisational adaptation and critical self-evaluation that some see as vital parts of public management (Metcalfe, 1991; Ranson and Stewart, 1989). Instead, we would see a mindless and debased 'managerialism' that does little credit to partnership or, indeed, to education.

POSTSCRIPT

This chapter was completed long before the publication of the government's White Paper, *Choice and Diversity: A New Framework for Schools* (Department for Education and Welsh Office, 1992) at the end of July 1992. The latter proposes changes for schooling in England and Wales that go far further towards diminishing the role and power of LEAs than do the 1988 reforms. The White Paper cannot be examined here, and instant comment is risky. Many have seen it as pronouncing the final death-sentence on LEAs, but some have noted that LEAs would still have an important part to play in relation to schools, parents and governors, and therefore have resources and influence, even apart from the new roles envisaged for them. The proposals do indeed strike a severe blow at LEAs, and prefigure their eventual demise. However, it may be as well to observe, firstly, that intentions are one thing, but legislation and its implementation over a long period are quite another. Secondly, that LEAs' life-expectancy – barring their forcible end, as happened with the Inner London Education Authority – depends only in part upon the rate of increase in the number of grant-maintained schools; also, that whilst that increase before 1995 will be a crucial determinant, it might well be less than the government expects, and very unevenly distributed. Thirdly, that although the relationship between LEAs and the proposed Funding Agency is unclear and unspecified, this dyarchy might well provide much scope for LEA influence and manoeuvre, in line with the argument of this chapter. Fourthly, that the Secretary of State for Scotland's early reaction was to eschew a similar line of development for Scotland. Fifthly, that the future shape of local government generally is also on the political agenda, and will itself exert a powerful but as yet indeterminate influence over the education service at the local level.

REFERENCES

Alexander, A. (1991) 'Managing Fragmentation: Democracy, Accountability and the Future of Local Government', *Local Government Studies*, 17(6): 63–76.

Audit Commission (1988) *Delegation of Management Authority to Schools*, London: HMSO.

Audit Commission (1989a) *Assuring Quality in Education: A Report on Local Authority Inspectors and Advisers*, (London: HMSO).

Audit Commission (1989b) *Losing an Empire, Finding a Role: The LEA of the Future*, London: HMSO.

Ball, S. (1990a) 'Education, Inequality and School Reform: Values in Crisis!' Inaugural Lecture, Centre for Educational Studies, King's College, University of London.

Ball, S. (1990b) *Politics and Policy Making in Education: Explorations in Policy Sociology*, London: Routledge.

Bogason, P. (1991) 'Control for Whom? Recent Advances in Research on Governmental Guidance and Control', *European Journal of Political Research* 20(2): 189–208.

Brooke, R. (1989) 'The Enabling Authority: Practical Consequences', *Local Government Studies* 15(5): 55–63.

Brooke, R. (1991) 'The Enabling Authority', *Public Administration* 69(4): 525–32.

Chitty, C. (1989) *Towards a New Education System: The Victory of the New Right?* London: Falmer.

Clarke, M. and Stewart, J. (1990) 'The Future of Local Government: Issues for Discussion', *Public Administration* 68(2): 249–58.

Coopers and Lybrand (1988) *Local Management of Schools: A Report to the Department of Education and Science*, London: HMSO.

Dale, R. (1989) *The State and Education Policy*, Milton Keynes: Open University Press.

Department for Education and Welsh Office (1992) *Choice and Diversity: A New Framework for Schools*, London: HMSO.

Department of the Environment (1991) *Local Government Review: The Structure of Local Government in England – A Consultation Paper*, London: Department of the Environment.

Dunsire, A. (1990) 'Holistic governance', *Public Policy and Administration* 5(1): 4–19.

Education Act 1980, London: HMSO.

Education (No. 2) Act 1986, London: HMSO.

Education Reform Act 1988, London: HMSO.

Education (Schools) Act 1992, London: HMSO.

Efficiency Unit (1988) *Improving Management in Government: The Next Steps*, London: HMSO.

Flude, M. and Hammer, M. (eds) (1990) *The Education Reform Act 1988: Its Origins and Implications*, London: Falmer.

Graham, N. (1965) 'The Administration of Education in Scotland', *Public Administration* 43(3): 299–311.

Griffith, J. (1966) *Central Departments and Local Authorities*, London: George Allen & Unwin.

Halpin, D., Power, S. and Fitz, J. (1992) 'Grant-maintained Schools: Making a Difference without Being Really Different', *British Journal of Educational Studies* 39(4): 409–24.

Hampton, W. (1991) *Local Government and Urban Politics* 2nd edn, London: Longman.

Hargreaves, D. and Reynolds, D. (eds) (1989) *Education Policies: Controversies and Critiques*, London: Falmer.

HMSO (1991) *The Citizen's Charter: Raising the Standard* Cm 1599, London: HMSO.

Hood, C. (1983) *The Tools of Government*, London: Macmillan.

Kean, H. (1991) 'Managing Education: The Local Authority Dimension', *Journal of Education Policy* 6(2): 145–54.

Kickert, W. (1991) 'Steering at a Distance: A New Paradigm of Public Governance in Dutch Higher Education', paper presented at the European Consortium for Political Research Joint Sessions of Workshops, University of Essex.

Kogan, M. (1987) 'Education', in Parkinson, M. (ed.) *Reshaping Local Government*, New Brunswick, NJ and Oxford: Policy Journals.

Kogan, M., Johnson, D., Packwood, T. and Whitaker, T. (1984) *School Governing Bodies*, London: Heinemann.

Lee, T. (1990) *Carving Out the Cash for Schools: LMS and the New ERA of Education*, Bath: Centre for the Analysis of Social Policy, University of Bath.

Local Government Training Board (1988) *Management in the Public Domain: A Discussion Paper*, Luton: Local Government Training Board.

Macbeth, A. (1990) *School Boards: From Purpose to Practice*, Edinburgh: Scottish Academic Press.

Maclure, S. (1988) *Education Re-formed: A Guide to the Education Reform Act*, London: Hodder & Stoughton.

McPherson, A. and Raab, C. (1988) *Governing Education: A Sociology of Policy since 1945*, Edinburgh: Edinburgh University Press.

Metcalfe, L. (1991) 'Public Management: From Imitation to Innovation', paper presented at the European Consortium for Political Research Joint Sessions of Workshops, University of Essex.

Metcalfe, L. and Richards, S. (1990) *Improving Public Management* 2nd edn, London: Sage.

Raab, C. (1992) 'Taking Networks Seriously: Education Policy in Britain', *European Journal of Political Research* 21(1–2): 69–90.

Raab, C. (forthcoming) 'Education', in Jordan, A. and Ashford, N. (eds) *Public Policy and the Impact of the New Right*, London: Pinter.

Ranson, S. (1990) 'From 1944 to 1988: Education, Citizenship and Democracy', in Flude, M. and Hammer, M. (eds) *The Education Reform Act 1988: Its Origins and Implications*, London: Falmer.

Ranson, S. and Stewart, J. (1989) 'Citizenship and Government: The Challenge for Management in the Public Domain', *Political Studies* 37(1): 5–24.

Rhodes, R. (1988) *Beyond Westminster and Whitehall: The Sub-Central Governments of Britain*, London: Unwin Hyman.

Scharpf, F. (1978) 'Interorganizational Policy Studies: Issues, Concepts and Perspectives', in Hanf, K. and Scharpf, F. (eds) *Interorganizational Policy Making: Limits to Coordination and Central Control*, London: Sage.

Schon, D. (1971) *Beyond the Stable State: Public and Private Learning in a Changing Society*, Harmondsworth: Penguin.

Simon, B. (1988) *Bending the Rules: The Baker 'Reform' of Education*, London: Lawrence & Wishart.

Thomas, G. (1991) 'Setting Up LMS', *Educational Management and Administration* 19(2): 84–8.

Thomas, G. and Levacic, R. (1991) 'Centralizing in order to Decentralize? DES Scrutiny and Approval of LMS Schemes', *Journal of Education Policy* 6(4): 401–16.

Thomas, H. (1990) 'From Local Financial Management to Local Management of Schools', in Flude, M. and Hammer, M. (eds) *The Education Reform Act 1988: Its Origins and Implications*, London: Falmer.

Wallace, M. (1991) 'Contradictory Interests in Policy Implementation: The Case of LEA Development Plans for Schools', *Journal of Education Policy* 6(4): 385–99.

Wallace, R. (1990) 'The Act and Local Authorities', in Flude, M. and Hammer, M. (eds) *The Education Reform Act 1988: Its Origins and Implications*, London: Falmer.

Walton, B. (1988) 'The Impact of the Government's Educational Legislation upon Local Government', *Local Government Studies* 14(1): 83–91.

Whitty, G. (1990) 'The New Right and the National Curriculum: State Control or Market Forces?' in Flude, M. and Hammer, M. (eds) *The Education Reform Act 1988: Its Origins and Implications*, London: Falmer.

Chapter 11

Conclusion

Pamela Munn

Three main themes have emerged in discussing the roles now assigned to parents as customers, managers and partners in their children's schooling. These are: school and teacher accountability for the educational experiences they offer; the tension between individual rights and collective rights in social policy; and the ideology of co-operation between parents and teachers in the school experience of individual children. This chapter looks at each of these themes and ends by speculating about the likely direction of parental involvement in schools in the future.

ACCOUNTABILITY

Ever since the state first gave grants to schools in 1833 it has wanted to ensure that schools were efficient, effective and providing value for money. Hence the establishment of Her Majesty's Inspectorate (HMI) in 1839 and, later, the infamous payment by results system. Current concern about accountability can be traced to James Callaghan's famous Ruskin College speech in 1976, where he linked Britain's declining economic performance with the failure of schools to raise standards sufficiently and their failure to teach about the importance of enterprise and the generation of wealth to the country's well-being. These sentiments were reiterated in a Consultative Paper, *Education in Schools* (1977).

After the Second World War British politicians had been more concerned with the accessibility of schooling than with the details of the school curriculum and school quality. While there had been concern about standards it was in the context of the two-tier system of secondary modern and grammar schools and the iniquities of the 11-plus examination, rather than the underperformance of schools. Callaghan's speech was a watershed, signalling government's concern with school performance in general, and in particular with its failure to deliver the skilled workforce seen as necessary for economic prosperity.

This concern was amplified by the Conservative government which succeeded the Labour administration in 1979. A series of 'Black Papers' had attacked school standards for being low and suggested that comprehensive schools were the cause. However, the attack on comprehensive schools was not confined to those on the British political right. Commentators of varying political, social and educational opinions were critical of what they saw as the failure of comprehensive schools to reduce inequalities of pupils' attainment associated with social economic status, to provide equality of educational opportunity and to manage resources effectively (e.g. Centre for Contemporary Cultural Studies, 1981; Cox and Marks, 1980; Hargreaves, 1982).

The demands for greater school accountability generated debate in academic circles about who should be accountable to whom about what. Responses ranged from Sockett (1976, 1980) who stressed the professional autonomy of teachers and advocated a system whereby they were accountable for their adherence to a code of conduct, to Elliot *et al.* (1981) who advocated 'democratic accountability', a process whereby schools would gradually open up the whole range of their activities to parents and the wider community and be responsive to their views on these activities. Many commentators highlighted the dangers of an 'output' model which stressed school accountability only in terms of measurable criteria such as pupil attainments or truancy rates.

Although there are many different views about what schools are accountable for, reflecting no doubt the vested interests of particular social groups, Rowbottom (quoted in Kogan, 1988: 3) offers a helpful definition of accountability as:

> a particular and concentrated responsibility of the individual for performance in keeping with the expectations of his own particular role. It implies the presence of a judge somewhere in the situation . . . armed with 'hard' institutional sanctions – the right to affect such things as pay, promotion, continued employment . . . as opposed to the softer sanction of generalised approval or reprobation possessed by all with whom the performer works.

Kogan makes the point that this definition also works for situations where more than one individual is called to account – a school, for instance – and where general rather than specific sanctions are available.

As I have argued elsewhere (Munn, 1991), if we take Rowbottom's definition of accountability as a starting point, and include in it rewards as well as sanctions, then three conditions (necessary but not in themselves sufficient) would need to be met for accountability to promote school improvement:

- a specification of the criteria which schools and/or teachers should try to meet
- a specification of the kinds of evidence which would indicate whether these criteria had been met
- the existence of knowledge about how to meet the specified criteria.

If accountability is a mechanism to improve schools, then judgements about school performance have to concern those aspects of school life which it is within a school's power to control. If schools have insufficient knowledge about how to improve performance, then it is unreasonable to expect them to improve.

The kinds of criteria against which schools are now explicitly or implicitly held to account are many and various. They include adherence to the national curriculum, pupil attainments, pupil attendance and provision of information about the school aims, homework, discipline policy and a wide range of other matters. It can be seen at once that some of these criteria are more entirely within a school's power to control than others. The provision of a school handbook or brochure setting out information about the school is almost entirely within the school's power to control, whereas a broad and balanced curriculum diet may be dependent on the school's ability to recruit teaching staff. Clearly, this is easier in some parts of Britain than others for reasons which have to do with living costs and general environmental factors as much as school recruitment procedures, or government's policies on teacher recruitment, supply and salaries. Further, a school's ability to meet certain criteria can be highly dependent on others fulfilling responsibilities. Perhaps the most obvious example of this is pupil attendance where legal responsibility lies with parents. Of course, schools have responsibility to promote regular attendance but condoned absence by parents is very difficult to combat.

Similarly, school effects on pupil attainments are not well understood, despite the growth in school effectiveness research. We are still in the realms of hypothesis testing and speculation in these matters.

SCHOOL ACCOUNTABILITY AND PARENTS

Schools have traditionally been accountable to local and central government. Local education authority advisers and HMI have been the agents of that accountability, although the criteria against which they evaluate schools have in the past not been made public. This is changing. The publication of performance indicators for schools and of school development plans is beginning to make explicit the kinds of criteria against which schools are to be judged. We can expect that these criteria will continue to be used with the emergence of private inspection companies south of the border. No such plans for private inspectors are, as yet, afoot in Scotland. Indeed, the largest region, Strathclyde, has established a quality assurance unit, with the clear remit of monitoring school performance and investigating possible under-achievement using a system called the 'Relative Rating Index' (Scottish Office Education Department, 1991) amongst others. Whoever does the inspection, it is clearly the government's intention that schools are inspected against national as well as local criteria.

Another new element in school accountability procedures is the enhanced role for parents in making sure that schools operate efficiently, effectively and provide value for money. Their role has been enhanced in two ways: through parental choice and through parental voice on governing bodies or school boards. Will these new roles lead to school improvement?

As far as parental choice is concerned, both Adler and Tomlinson have pointed out that choice is not a practical proposition for a number of parents. They live in areas where there is in reality no alternative to their local school or, in the case of ethnic minority parents in some London boroughs, where they have no choice because school places are not available. Where parents do exercise choice, they choose schools on criteria such as geographical location, safety features or the kind of children who already attend. These are not criteria to which 'loser' schools can easily respond. Whether pupils' educational attainments have been increased through choice is an empirical question to which we do not yet know the answer.

Parental voice opens up, in my opinion, greater possibilities for school improvement than parental choice. Through involving parents more directly in school affairs, school governorship increases opportunities for a better knowledge and understanding of school life and for influencing school developments. Golby and Munn describe the experience of governing bodies and school boards, each highlighting the possibilities for promoting local democracy through active citizenship. There is tangible evidence of this through local and national federations of school boards in Scotland and most tellingly by parental opposition to government policy on national testing. Scottish local and central government have become more accountable to boards in the sense of having to explain and defend their policies. Improvements to schools as a result have tended to be in terms of improvements to school buildings, or safer access through provision of supervised places to cross busy roads. Such improvements can be regarded as marginal by some commentators but, in the context of a climate where most schools are seen to be doing a good job, are important achievements entirely consistent with parental criteria of school choice. It is still too early to say what the future holds for governing bodies or boards and whether they will become actively involved in monitoring teaching quality. There are already considerable demands on their time and they may well be reluctant to add to their duties.

INDIVIDUAL WELFARE AND COLLECTIVE WELFARE

'Social welfare programmes typically provide benefits and services to clients in ways that are intended to promote collective welfare' (Adler *et al.*, 1989: 1). In other words, such programmes are intended to serve a dual function: to help the individual in need and to do so in ways which promote the general well-being of society. These are difficult and sometimes irreconcilable goals for social and economic policy but goals nevertheless which few politicians would eschew. For example, a change in the personal taxation system which disproportionately benefited the wealthy was presented by a Conservative Chancellor of the Exchequer and others in terms of its general benefits to economic growth and 'trickle down' effects which would advantage the whole society.

In schooling there has been a marked shift away from a collective welfare orientation (ensuring equality of access to comprehensive schools) towards an individual client orientation. The rights of individual clients – that is, of – parents have begun to assume greater prominence. The implications of this are discussed by Jonathan, Macbeth, Adler and Tomlinson. The dominance of a parent's right to choose the school attended by his or her children has important consequences for schooling as a collective welfare right which we need to consider in evaluating this shift towards the rights of individual clients. The potential benefits to the numbers of parents who have exercised their right to choose have to be weighed against the potential impact on schooling as a service from which society should benefit. What are the costs and benefits? Those parents exercising choice are, no doubt, pleased to do so and believe they have gained an advantage for their children. Furthermore, choice is available to a wider range of parents than those who, in the past, exercised choice by buying a house in the catchment area of their preferred school. These benefits carry potentially high costs. Firstly, it can reduce the range of choice open to succeeding generations of parents. 'As unpopular schools close and the number of surplus places in the system are reduced, then the range of choices available to parents actually contracts' (Ball, 1990: 4). And as Macbeth points out, one generation of parents can opt a school out of local authority control for succeeding generations. Secondly, as pressure mounts on popular schools, these schools could choose parents rather than vice versa, and if pupil attainment is the criterion on which schools become increasingly accountable to government, there may well be a reluctance to admit low-attaining pupils and pupils who have statements or records of special educational needs. These pupils would lower the school's attainment record. Thirdly, where the individual client orientation of parental choice supercedes other legislation such as the Race Relations Act, the goal of multicultural school provision is challenged. Fourthly, the notion that members of the community other than parents have a legitimate interest in schooling is played down.

Adler suggests ways forward, maintaining a different balance between individual client and collective welfare orientation but recognising the legitimacy of parental choice. He points to the need to offer some protection to under-enrolled schools suffering from a bandwagon effect of parental choice, to encourage diversity of provision and alongside this for parents to use educational criteria in choosing schools, that is, to make a case on the grounds of the particular and distinctive educational opportunities offered by one school rather than another. These might be in terms of teaching methods, special curriculum provision or particular aspects of school ethos. Such an approach is not without its problems but, within a framework of schooling as a collective welfare right, it does offer a way of preserving a parent's right to choose.

PARENT–TEACHER CO-OPERATION

Partnership has been a theme touched on by most contributors whether in terms of national and local level policy-making or in terms of home–school, parent–teacher relations. Golby, Bastiani and Raab offer different interpretations of the term, while Hegarty believes it is not a useful construct in thinking about home–school relations. Partners come in different shapes and sizes. It is curious that much of the writing on home–school partnership projects emphasises ways of developing 'more *equal* relationships between the home and school' [added emphasis] (e.g. Royal Society of Arts, 1991: 1). If one equates education with schooling, then it is questionable whether parents could be equal partners with teachers, since they are unlikely to possess the same level of skills, knowledge and expertise. If, on the other hand, schooling is seen as part of education, then teachers are likely to be junior partners. Macbeth points out how small a proportion of a child's learning takes place in school. Indeed, Leichter (1985), argues that education in families cannot necessarily be improved by attempting to make it more like school. Rather, local and national education policy should take into account the rich and varied processes by which education takes place in families.

Clearly, parents and teachers have a common interest in their children's schooling, wanting it to be happy, productive and effective. The majority of teachers and parents share the same broad goals for their children and each party brings complementary skills and expertise. Teachers have expertise in pedagogy, subject knowledge, and the demands of curriculum and of assessment, for example. Parents provide a learning environment for children in which much is transmitted: cultural capital as well as a place to do homework. Macbeth draws attention to the need for a 'paradigm shift' on the part of teachers if they are to work more effectively with parents. But a paradigm shift is also needed for parents, to recognise the legitimacy and value of their own contribution to their children's schooling and the validity of their point of view. In this context, partnership means a shared commitment to means and ends, a joint understanding of the realistic and attainable goals for individual pupils, how these are to be achieved and the respective parts which teachers, parents and pupils will play in this process. Procedures for resolving differences have to be worked out, of course, but the paradigm shift is required of both teachers and parents, teachers recognising that parents have legitimate interests in the goals set for their children and parents recognising that they have such a role to play however expert and knowledgeable teachers are.

It is noteworthy that where the child is seen as heavily dependent, for example in the infant school, or has pronounced special educational needs, teachers and parents usually see a need to work together in the best interests of the child. This is perhaps because it is easier to define specific goals or targets for pupils, even though neither party may think of them in quite that way. For infants there are targets for reading, counting, tying shoelaces, socialising with other children and so on which are taken for granted and largely uncontroversial. Hegarty illustrates similar phenomena in discussing parent–teacher communication in the context of children with special educational needs. Teacher–parent communication in such circumstances is typically frequent, regular and informal. Teachers still tend to call the shots as far as school values are concerned, but it seems generally to be accepted that part of the proper professional role for teachers in these circumstances is direct and frequent communication with parents – an acceptance that parents are a valuable source of information about the child's attainment, progress and attitudes.

This attitude changes as children progress through primary and secondary school. This may be partly because the curriculum becomes less familiar to parents and so they are readier to accept teachers' goals for their children. This needs to change. It will be interesting to know if parents take a more active role in discussing curriculum goals with teachers under the national curriculum framework which specifies targets and levels of achievement and if they are readier to discuss the teaching methods used to help children attain goals. However, better mechanisms of home–school communication are needed as well as a change in attitude. Research indicates that parents have a good deal of trust in teachers' professional expertise and competence (e.g. Johnson, 1991; Munn *et al.*, 1982; Wolfendale, 1989). Consequently, at parents' evenings they are reluctant to challenge a teacher's opinion or account of their child's behaviour and progress. In any event, such an account, usually taking a few minutes and often given within the hearing of other parents, was seen as unsatisfactory and not worth the effort of re-arranging shifts or losing earnings which can often be the cost to working-class parents of attending. Instead, children become the best sources of information of what is happening at school. They are seen as in touch with the mysteries of subject options and the school culture in a much more expert way than parents. Furthermore, Johnson (1991) found that parents look for signs that young people are preparing to assume responsibility for their own lives and that home–school communication or negotiation that bypasses the students may be seen as detrimental by parents. Thus teachers' preconceptions that parents who do not turn up to parents' evenings are not interested in their children's schooling, can be mistaken. Given the circumstances described above it can be an entirely rational choice for parents and indeed the wonder is that so many turn up at all.

It seems that a 'paradigm shift' is necessary by both parents and teachers to transform traditional home–school relations from the home's unquestioning support of the school's way of doing things. Many experiments in home–school partnerships are now under way in various parts of Britain, some of them reported in this book. These are often uncoordinated and go unreported. Better dissemination spelling out the time, effort and other resources needed to transform home–school relations and indications of the benefits would help. However, improved mechanisms of contact and additional home visiting staff will not by themselves lead to better relations without teachers and parents being aware of the assumptions each brings to interaction and a determination to change them.

FINALLY . . .

This chapter has suggested that parents as managers and partners probably hold out greater prospects for school improvement than parents as customers. Yet the policy framework in which parents and teachers operate profoundly influences their relations. Formula funding with a school budget firmly fixed to pupil numbers does not augur well for free and frank collaboration between teachers and parents over their children's schooling. Popular schools might become complacent, unwilling to reflect critically on the educational experience they are offering children, as long as they continue to attract customers. Relationships among teachers in the same school can also be affected by national policy. Ball (1990) reports that ordinary teachers can feel distanced from senior staff preoccupied with financial targets and budgets rather than the school curriculum, discipline and the usual trappings of school life. It would be a pity if the opportunities for greater parental involvement in schools through governing bodies and home–school partnerships were constrained by market forces.

Parents now have an opportunity to influence school policy as never before. In Scotland parental opposition to national testing has been vocal, and in England and Wales parents have expressed their disquiet about Conservative government plans to 'privatise' school inspections. Parents are becoming a force to be reckoned with in the constellation of interests which play a role in policy formation and implementation. Let us hope that the positive teacher–parent relations evident on macro-policy issues can be replicated in individual parent–teacher consultation and nego-tiation about the school experience of individual children.

REFERENCES

Adler, M., Petch, A. and Tweedie, J. (1989) *Parental Choice and Educational Policy*, Edinburgh: Edinburgh University Press.

Ball, S. (1990) 'Education, Inequality and School Reform: Values in Crisis!' Inaugural Lecture, Centre for Educational Studies, King's College, University of London.

Centre for Contemporary Cultural Studies (1981) *Unpopular Education: Schooling and Social Democracy in England and Wales since 1944*, London: Hutchinson.

Cox, C. and Marks, J. (1980) *Real Concern*, London: Centre for Policy Studies.

Education in Schools: A Consultative Document (1977) Cmnd 6869, London: HMSO.

Elliot, J., Bridges, D., Ebbutt, D., Gibson, R. and Nias, J. (1981) *School Accountability*, London: Grant McIntyre.

Hargreaves, D. (1982) *The Challenge for the Comprehensive School*, London: Routledge & Kegan Paul.

Johnson, D. (1991) 'Parents, Students and Teachers: A Three-Way Relationship', *International Journal of Educational Research* 15(2): 171–81.

Kogan, M. (1988) *Educational Accountability: An Analytic Overview*, London: Hutchinson.

Leichter, H.J. (1985) 'Families as Educators', in Fantini, M. and Sinclair, R. (eds) *Education in School and Non-School Settings* Eighty-fourth Yearbook of the National Society for the Study of Education part I, Chicago: Chicago University Press.

Munn, P. (1991) 'School Boards, Accountability and Control', *British Journal of Educational Studies* 39(2): 173–89.

Munn, P., Hewitt, G., Morrison, A. and McIntyre, D. (1982) *Accountability and Professionalism* (Educational Monograph No. 10), Stirling: Education Department, University of Stirling.

Royal Society of Arts (1991) *The Home–School Contract of Partnership: Summary Report*, London: Royal Society of Arts.

Scottish Office Education Department (1991) *The School Relative Rating Index*, Edinburgh: HMSO.

Sockett, H. (1976) 'Teacher Accountability', *Proceedings of the Philosophy of Education Society* 10 (July): 34–57.

Sockett, H. (1980) 'Accountability: The Contemporary Issues', in Sockett, H. (ed.) *Accountability in the English Education System*, London: Hodder & Stoughton.

Wolfendale, S. (ed.) (1989) *Parental Involvement: Developing Networks between School, Home and Community*, London: Cassell.

Index